The Trivialization of
the United Presbyterian Church

JOHN R. FRY

The
Trivialization
of the
United
Presbyterian
Church

Harper & Row, Publishers
New York
Evanston
San Francisco
London

Quotations from *The Confession of 1967* © 1966 by the General Assembly, United Presbyterian Church, U.S.A. are used by permission.

THE TRIVIALIZATION OF THE UNITED PRESBYTERIAN CHURCH. Copyright © 1975 by John R. Fry. All rights reserved. Printed in the United States of America. No part of this book may be used or reproduced in any manner whatsoever without written permission except in the case of brief quotations embodied in critical articles and reviews. For information address Harper & Row, Publishers, Inc., 10 East 53rd Street, New York, N.Y. 10022. Published simultaneously in Canada by Fitzhenry & Whiteside Limited, Toronto.

FIRST EDITION

Library of Congress Cataloging in Publication Data

Fry, John R
    The trivialization of the United Presbyterian Church.

    Includes bibliographical references.
    1. United Presbyterian Church—Doctrinal and controversial works. I. Title.
BX8955.F79   1975   285'.131   75–9319
ISBN 0–06–063074–4

75 76 77 78 79 10 9 8 7 6 5 4 3 2 1

To Religion's Cultured Despisers:
You are right.

Preface

The material argument of the foregoing essay speaks for itself but I do owe the reader three pieces of information which are not contained in the essay; they are extraneous to the essay but important to know before reading it.

First, I have concentrated attention on publicly available materials. In a few places I use material gathered in interviews with knowledgable individuals but I use it for the purpose of clarifying a murkiness in the public record. This material plays no crucial role in the essay. The important material comes from the public domain. The trivialization of the United Presbyterian Church is not like Watergate, where important material had to be dug out of private sources. This didn't happen behind closed doors; it happened out in the open.

I could have written a very different kind of essay, in fact a very long book, brimming over with my own private recollection and the recollection of most of the principals in recent Presbyterian history. It would have been a scandalously vindictive book. The reader deserves to know that I deliberately did not write such a book and why. The reason is simple. It would not have answered the basic question I think needs answering. Which is: What ever happened to the United Presbyterian Church? And the reason a lot of subjective discharge would not answer the question is that the principals themselves don't know what ever happened to the United Presbyterian

vii

Church. They know a lot of inside stories, but they don't know the outside story—the important one. And practically the whole membership of the denomination joins them in that ignorance.

Second, I conceive the basic question to be rather more theological than merely historical. I have therefore constructed the essay along theological lines. Here is what I mean. I focus a lot of attention on the decision to give *reconciliation* a central position in a modern confession of faith in order to show how this decision was then used to justify a thoroughgoing reorganization, as though the reorganization actually had a theological mandate, along the lines of "God is calling us to reorganize." For me that is a directly theological matter. I argue that God was calling Presbyterians to attend to the requirements of faithfulness placed on a modern, complex, national ecclesiastical institution—and still is. The decision to reorganize obscured the main theological matter—and still does. I do not hear God calling the church to become a first-century church or to model itself after a business organization or a government. I hear God calling the church to undertake the works of love and justice as an institution among other institutions in a modern world. Since God has not changed the modern world back into a nineteenth-century world or a first-century world, there is all the more reason to be serious about both love and justice in the only world there is, as the institution the United Presbyterian Church certainly is.

I have been arguing along these lines for a long time. I was a practicing middle level Presbyterian bureaucrat for ten years almost, then a pastor in a besieged ghetto for six years, and most recently have been teaching social ethics in a Presbyterian seminary. Whether before the Board of Christian Education, *Presbyterian Life* magazine, the Presbytery of Chicago, a Senate investigating committee, a congregation, or a seminar, I have made the same theological argument. I think the reader deserves to know that before taking up the essay. It is an argument. It is intended to show not only *that* the United Presbyterian Church has been backing out of the domain of "principalities and powers" as fast as it can, but why. If the essay stirs up latent Presbyterian tendencies to recommence representing the claims of love and justice in that big bad world out there, that will be an unforeseen bonus. If it operates as a moral lesson for non-Presbyterians, many of whom are beginning to evade their theological summonses by entering a long reorganizational parenthesis of their own, I'll take that as a bonus too.

Third, I have noticed a definite recent tendency in the commentary of big-time church historians and other Protestant "voices" considered major enough to explain the recent Protestant past. This is a tendency to lump all the churches together as "mainline churches." Thus Baptists, Methodists, Episcopalians, members of the United Church of Christ, Lutherans, members of the Reformed Church of America, and Presbyterians are found to be so similar that their differences are insignificant. This is a very useful procedure, if the purpose is to present this group of Christians as the old liberal establishment fuddy-duds, the better to contrast them with new-now Christian enthusiasts who *really* love, speak in tongues, heal the sick, sing gospel songs, and otherwise revel in religious experience: clearly the absolute wave of the future. But while useful, this procedure is also fraudulent. Religious enthusiasm is not a new phenomenon on the face of the earth. That a lot of Americans currently are indulging in it can more easily be explained as a failure of nerve than as a sudden taste for pure religion. When highly placed, influential, and quotable "voices" move onto the obviously *safe* ground of repudiating the liberal excesses of the sixties the better to celebrate the religious enthusiasm of the seventies, skepticism just naturally begins to flourish.

The Protestant denominations have been thrown together for the convenience of critical disparagement. That is the meaning of *mainline churches.* The story line behind the very use of the expression is inevitable. The mainline churches messed around with politics; got too far out in front on racial issues; were too outspoken against the Vietnam war; were captured by radicals; confused social action with religion; became secularized; and so on. Too bad for them. They are finished. That is what stands behind the use of the expression *mainline churches.* I therefore resist the use of the expression, the simplistic story line behind it, and the nomination of a tiny ripple as the wave of the future.

Each of the major American denominations has its own specific tradition no less than its own particular recent history. Accordingly, I have not written about *all* Protestants, or *all* Christians, or *all* religious people because this procedure inhibits the development of real understanding of a particular tradition and denominational history. I focus on United Presbyterians. It is my own witness against current popular trends—for what it is worth. I hope that non-Presbyterian readers will see the point of that and will begin an equally intense and focused study of their own recent past. Non-Presbyterian readers, at any rate, should know in advance why I have dealt with their particular situations so rarely. I hope some of them will write essays on their own situations from which Presbyterians can learn.

I

The Reconciliation Decision

The initials UPCUSA stand for the United Presbyterian Church
in the U.S.A.—a union of two denominations in 1958: the United
Presbyterian Church in North America and the Presbyterian Church
in the U.S.A. This UPCUSA[1] began its long downhill slide into
mediocrity at the exact moment some of the best minds in the church
decided to make reconciliation the center and organizing theme of
a contemporary confession of faith. The date is not important.
Whenever made, that decision began to produce consequences,
which immediately began to produce consequences of their own,
and so on until, a decade later, the denomination acts like a faded
country club which must raise assessments on its members again or
sell the property and quit. The decision itself didn't produce the
downfall, but it made the downfall possible and probably inevitable.
This rendering of history places a lot of importance on an intellectual
decision. Those present-day Presbyterians who want to understand
their situation as some crisis or other that they can shortly work out
of will no doubt consider this kind of account absurd. They don't
think intellectual decisions amount to much.

The minds I refer to belong to the fifteen illustrious Presbyterians
who were chosen as the Special Committee on a Brief Contemporary
Statement of Faith. It was a high-powered committee, composed of
eight professors, four pastors, and three bureaucrats, among them

the lone woman. Conceding for the moment the existence of a liberal establishment in the denomination, these fifteen would be counted solid, even renowned, members, given neither to rashness nor cowardice. Accordingly, their decision was thought solid though novel—and, it turns out, disastrous. They were good-ol' boys plus one good-ol'-boy woman, so they must have known what they were doing, even though it was unusual.

The ancient creeds of the Christian church and the confessions framed in the Protestant Reformation are organized around the being of God—the persons of the trinity, for instance, or the attributes of God's being, such as sovereignty, righteousness, faithfulness, and so on. This modern Presbyterian confession was organized around what God has *done* (the reconciling work) and what God calls the church *to do* (the mission of reconciliation). The various materials of a regular confession of faith all still get in but are fit into an action-centered structure. Henceforth, if you want to know who God is, then look at what God does; if you want to know what the church is, then look at what the church is commanded to do and in that light consider what the church says it does or says it should do.

From one angle the decision looks downright modern. What could be more modern than the assumption that doing is the occasion for the disclosure of being?[2] That is the wrong angle. The authors of the confession saw in reconciliation, as Karl Barth had so ably taught them, the positive and comprehensive disclosure of God's judgment and grace. Removed from the 850 or so toiling commissioners at some General Assembly who would eventually vote for the thing, the decision looks like it could have been made on intellectual grounds alone, that is, Is it true? and Is it biblical? According to Professor Edward Dowey, Jr., the chairman of the committee, it was just that kind of decision. He explains in his *Commentary on the Confession of 1967*[3] that "reconciliation is one of the rare terms in the Bible that can epitomize the whole gospel in one word." The written-out and voted-for eventual confession[4] reads:

> God's reconciling work in Jesus Christ and the mission of reconciliation to which he has called his church are the heart of the gospel in any age.

Reconciliation fills the bill, if a single-term, condensed statement of the gospel is required. The novelty of the decision and the explanation Dowey provides in his commentary arises at that point. What is the good of any single term? The *gospel,* or what they call the gospel, is the entire New Testament plus twenty centuries of reflection and commentary, plus what reverent imagination might supply any minute now. There is enough diffusion in the gospel to raise a question about an attempt to jam it all into a single term. It had to be that very term, *reconciliation,* and not some other single term that tipped the decision. The drafting committee didn't likely rifle the pages of the New Testament in search of any single and rare term, or, if they did, they would never have discovered that

Our generation stands in peculiar need of reconciliation in Christ.[5]

In the view of the drafting committee, as it surveyed the gospel and the world, reconciliation means the positive conclusion of fighting, and not a temporary cease-fire. It is the settling of differences in the context of a rediscovered mutuality. Maybe that is also what the New Testament means by reconciliation, but it is certainly what liberal Americans believed in the early sixties. With liberals everywhere in retreat and none too sure they are or were liberals then, and with every week's mail bringing a fresh batch of articles and notices of books on the subject of what in the world happened to the liberals, and especially with the radical left smashing liberals for having been lackeys of the system all along, it is going to be hard to get this word in edgewise. But I shall try. Liberals were timid in the early sixties. They didn't like fighting. They liked to argue and also to vote, particularly in confused parliamentary situations, but only slightly less than they liked to meet and write things for the paper. They tended to want to retire from real fights. This may not describe all liberals accurately, but the liberals I have come to know in the UPCUSA were that way.

The liberal drafting committee expressed something bordering on reverence for reconciliation. It is the all-purpose ending to all the trouble in the world. Reconciliation comprises in itself all the world could be and, from the side of the gospel, should be. It is the answer provided by God to the modern world through the Presbyterian church. It is also the answer provided by practically every morally sensitive and probably liberal American anguished by the mounting violence of national life. They seemed to think any kind of negotiation, or compromise, or trade-off is preferable to the use of violence to resolve conflict. With them any peace seemed better than any war —across the board, always.

Reconciliation proves to be an architectonic marvel, reciprocating relevance *to* the gospel and the relevance *of* the gospel to the modern world. Very well, what is this vaunted reconciliation, aside from the reconciliation-as-stop-the-fighting which the modern mind already knows? This comes out in the confession itself as a three-part theory. Probably the drafting committee would object to the use of the word *theory.* They prepared a statement which, once approved by the denomination, became a confession of *faith,* that is, a confession of belief that the materials are true in themselves as something like facts. But before being adopted, the materials prepared by the committee were not yet articles of faith, so can be considered a theory without unduly offending Presbyterian sensibilities and should be considered a theory in the presence of those many readers, including not a few Presbyterians, who are not prepared to certify theoretical constructions as fact, yet.

The reconciliation theory begins with the church looking back through the eyes of the New Testament at the crucifixion-resurrection of Jesus Christ, the grand spectacle of reconciliation. God discloses himself in Jesus Christ.[6] God was doing something. He was making the FIRST MOVE to overcome a tremendous alienation between himself and mankind. Mankind can't make the first move toward God, owing to its sin and rebellious spirit; the point is more that mankind wouldn't make the first move because of a poisoned will. Left to itself, mankind would have smashed itself up on the rocks of its own sin, but God did not leave mankind to itself. God took on himself mankind's own death in order to affirm the divine decision in favor of mankind's life. It was a decision which had cosmic reverberations because it involved the alteration of cosmic structures.

God's intention was to reestablish fellowship with his alienated creature—mankind; the corollary intention was to reestablish fellowship within mankind itself. The crucifixion-resurrection is therefore not merely good cosmic theater—to dramatize unforgettably God's love for mankind—but also represents a definite shift in the divine attitude and a decision to go to the lengths of allowing his Son to die and rearranging the cosmos for the purpose of doing something about this sin-as-alienation.

Reconciliation is a costly activity, requiring death in its supreme instance; its natural foe is sin. Exacerbating conflict is the work of sin; thus, reconciliation goes through the shadow of sin in the conflict to the sin itself. The stubborn maintenance of differences fuels conflict. Reconciliation seeks to dissolve the stubborness—the pride—and in that way brings the parties of a conflict to agreeable restoration of mutuality. The natural scene of reconciliation is the inwardness of hostility backed up by a poisoned will. Reconciliation has no alternative. It must risk the attack of hostility in order to overcome it.

As Presbyterians came later to base ecclesiastical action on C-67,[7] they pictured reconciliation as some mere patching up of differences of opinion. It should be emphasized that the confession's theory of reconciliation would not allow that kind of construction. Reconciliation does not patch; it plunges.

The second part of the theory of reconciliation deals with the formation of the church. In accordance with the realigned cosmos and energized by the restoration of fellowship with God—"filled with the Spirit"—some human beings directly after the crucifixion-resurrection began to make some "first moves" on their own for the purpose of overcoming alienation within mankind. They said God had picked them to be the "piled up ones," that is, the church. They had a special two-fold task in life: to tell mankind what God had done and to do the first moving so that mankind could see what God had in mind. A peculiarly intense instance of alienation at the time the church was forming was the enmity between Jews and Gentiles. The church, led by the Spirit to see that this enmity had been already overcome by God, went about replacing the enmity with brotherhood in Christ. In other words, there was no barrier, *that God could see,* to Jews believing in Christ. This was the first known instance of abolishing anti-Semitism by giving Semites the opportunity to become Gentiles. At any rate, when there is alienating conflict, someone has to make a first move, to take the plunge, to risk all in order to undo the work of sin. The church was formed for the express purpose of witnessing to this truth and, furthermore, doing this truth.

This does not complete the reconciliation theory; the first two parts are a ground for the theory's completion in the present. The God who made the reconciling first move in Jesus Christ is still making the first move in the modern world. The church still has the same mission to do the work of reconciliation and to bear the message of reconciliation to the world, with one important difference. After twenty centuries, it is not so much lack of hearing about reconciliation that is the world's need but a lack of seeing what the message amounts to. Accordingly, the modern church seems to be under a refined mandate to do rather more working at reconciliation than talking about it, which reverses the order of the first church; it featured itself as being empowered to preach rather more than to do.

The requirements made on the theory as a whole are relatively simple. It must take adequate account of the New Testament and ancient theological authorities of the church and that is all. The theory need not make sense to the general everybody in the world. It does not have to document God's first moves in the modern world, for instance, hidden as they are under a secular disguise. As long as Presbyterians know God is working, that closes the matter: he *is* working. There are straight-line connections that faith recognizes between the crucifixion-resurrection and the panorama of blood-soaked modern life. In fact, the materials of modern life take on the primary characteristic of being items in the history of reconciliation. History is cruciform, dominated by the reconciling work of God in Jesus Christ.

The developed theory of reconciliation renews attention on the reconciliation decision itself. The drafting committee did more than organize a confession. They installed reconciliation as the name of life, the name of the church, and the name of God. Reconciliation begins to appear as a substantial metaphysical (cosmic) force in its own right. Yes, reconciliation stands for God in Christ, but the confession makes it stand independently. God does nothing in this confession. "In his reconciling love he overcomes . . ." and "God's reconciliation is the ground of . . ." and "The reconciliation of man through Jesus Christ makes it plain . . ." and "The reconciling word of the gospel is God's judgment . . ." There is no plain old God; it is always God-as or God-in or God-through.

Were the Brief Statement of Contemporary Faith a rousement to enthuse Presbyterians or a piece of theological instruction for the church, the novelty of the reconciliation decision could be admired or quarreled with along strictly intellectual lines. The importance of the decision is tied to the fact that this confession in time was added to the major creeds and confessions of the Christian church and enjoys similar standing. Furthermore, the brief statement, once ratified, became an authority to be appealed to in clarifying ecclesiastical policy. It can simply be assumed that as Presbyterians in the past found justification for their policies in the Westminster Confession of Faith (whether it was there or not made little difference if it seemed to be there), Presbyterians after 1967 went scurrying to the new confession for ammunition or support or both. Willy-nilly, a confession of faith is a linguistic legacy.

The intellectual ingredients of the reconciliation decision do not go along with the confession as a permanent sort of explanation. Once made, the decision produces a document, and the document will ever after be explained by just about any Presbyterian who can read and wants to explain it. And if explanations differ, that is what reconciliation is all about, isn't it? To iron out those differences. Suddenly the central placement of reconciliation becomes important. With reconciliation as the operative authority of the confession, Presbyterians can't really fight over the confession, or fight over fighting, and anyone win. There are no sure ways to determine the validity of the differences. That is the bottom line.

The Politics of the Reconciliation Decision

It is easy to believe that the fifteen people who made the reconciliation decision had a few political things on their minds as well as strictly intellectual considerations. Students of creed-making in the history of the Christian church would assume these political elements as a matter of course. Behind the actual intention to clarify faith, students find, there is an intention to cleanse faith. This was true, for instance, in the formulation of the so-called Apostles' Creed, which set down orthodox apostolic faith in unforgettable form and also declared the Gnostic Christians—about one-third of the whole second-century church—heretics. That was the political element. The Nicene Creed, similarly, clarified the divine-human status of Jesus Christ and also got the Arian Christians classified as heretics. Even the Barmen Confession, made by German Evangelicals in 1934, hammered away at the regular German Christians for submitting to ecclesiastical protocols promulgated by the Third Reich.[8]

The political elements of C-67, which creed study would almost presuppose, are linked with the intellectual elements so strongly that it could seem they played some part in the actual decision—as maybe the basic intention. The political elements are explicit and appear in the section of the confession entitled, "Reconciliation in Society." In his pony, Dowey explains,[9]

> The gospel and the mission of reconciliation swing the sensitized church like a compass needle to the troubled places (of society) where its message and deeds are most needed.

This is a revealing explanation. The church is a pure doing, pointed, or rather, swung here and there by reconciliation, without another thought about it. But look now at the areas of specific need in society reconciliation has swung the sensitized needle of a Presbyterian church toward: racial warfare, international strife, poverty, and sexual anarchy. As pure doing, the church, once positioned, moves into these areas as commissioned, not even thinking about the stubborn fact that the UPCUSA (as doing, resisting, undoing, arguing, retreating, advancing, and sleeping) had been debating that very subject at every General Assembly for a decade. Dowey has a nice down-home way of ignoring the significant portion of the denomination that on any given specific social area will be automatically pointed in the other direction as vibrantly as the sensitized church is pointing in the reconciliation-indicated direction. So what is to be made of that pointing differential? The confession's answer is unequivocal. "Off with their heads!" This is a thoroughly predictable answer from the standpoint of creed-study but odd in a confession celebrating the centrality of reconciliation in the Christian faith.

The language of the confession should be followed closely at just this point.[10]

RACIAL WARFARE

> God has created the peoples of the earth to be one universal family. In his reconciling love he overcomes the barriers between brothers and breaks down every form of discrimination based on racial or ethnic difference, real or imaginary. . . . Therefore the church labors for the abolition of all racial discrimination and ministers to those injured by it.

So far, so good. No problems here. But then out of the zone of the clearly unexpected comes something very close—or as close as Presbyterians can get—to an anathema.

> Congregations, or groups of Christians who exclude, dominate, or patronize their fellowmen, however subtly, resist the Spirit of God and bring contempt on the faith which they profess.

Dowey remarks that this is not an anathema but is the church confessing to itself.[11] It is possible.

INTERNATIONAL STRIFE

God's reconciliation is the ground of the peace, justice, and freedom among nations which all powers of government are called to serve and defend. The church, in its own life, is called to practice the forgiveness of enemies and to command to the nations as practical politics, the search for cooperation and peace.

Again, there is nothing objectionable in the statement this far. It is about equal to the scout law in controversial content. The authors push on, however, into a genuinely explosive area.

This requires the pursuit of fresh and responsible relations across every line of conflict, *even at the risk to national security,* to reduce areas of strife and to broaden international understanding.

The adverbial phrase I have italicized came to be the most well-known part of the confession because it represented most clearly the theological price the confessors had attached to being counted a solid Presbyterian believer. It seemed to oblige Christians to honor peace above national security, which duplicates the Communist line, for one thing, in the minds of many Presbyterians, and was thought to be a needless display of antipatriotism. For these Presbyterians the price was too high and recklessly attached.

POVERTY

The reconciliation of man through Jesus Christ makes it plain that enslaving poverty in a world of alienation is an intolerable violation of God's good creation. Because Jesus identified himself with the needy and exploited, the cause of the world's poor is the cause of his disciples.

With which there would have been near perfect concurrence had the matter been left right there. It wasn't. The confession now moves into some choice and unmistakable condemnation.

A church that is indifferent to poverty, or evades responsibility in economic affairs, or is open to one social class only, or expects gratitude for its beneficence makes a mockery of reconciliation and offers no acceptable worship to God.

An explorer would have been hard-pressed to find even 10 percent of the particular congregations in the denomination which

9

could read that statement without flinching or, worse, bristling. The UPCUSA is upper-middle-class, largely white, economically conservative, and expert at extracting the last ounce of gratitude possible for the smallest show of beneficence to the poor. There was little point in disputing the condemnation because it was true on its face. But why was it formulated this way? Why was no thought given to the people trapped in single-class suburban ghettos?

SEXUAL ANARCHY

> Anarchy in sexual relationships is a symptom of man's alienation from God, his neighbor, and himself. . . . The church, as the household of God, is called to lead men out of this alienation into the responsible freedom of the new life in Christ.

Insofar as the confession discusses the well-known crack-up of the family, or the drastic rise in open promiscuity, or, between the cracks, the first stirrings of a proud homosexuality, which it seems to be doing, there is no problem. The church was ready and willing to condemn these things all day long, but it doesn't turn out that way.

> The church comes under the judgment of God and invites rejection by man when it fails to lead men and women into the full meaning of life together, or withholds the compassion of Christ from those caught in the moral confusion of our time.

In other words, duck!

The apparently gratuitous denunciations at the end of each of the four specific social areas are daggers thrown at the heart of the conservative, old-fashioned, racist, superpatriotic, snobbish, and sexually hung-up. The theory comes first, then the hit. To the force of reason is then added the force of theological opprobrium. Henceforth, if you believe God was in Christ reconciling the world to himself, and if you believe God gave a mission of reconciliation to the church, and if you believe God still means the church to do his will, you people out there will all begin acting like regular liberal Democrats.

The conclusion is irresistible. The drafting committee apparently believed that reconciliation, standing there in its compelling wonder, would transform the denomination into a unified beehive of mission activity. Or else, the committee used reconciliation like a club to beat the brains out of the reconciliation-poops. In either case, the reconciliation decision was bad politics. It must be considered either insensitive, hence arrogant, or abstract-theological, hence arrogant. Had there been a focused concern to present the great theological issues facing the church in those days—concerning the distinctive responsibility of an independent ecclesiastical institution to contest major public issues with other financial and governmental institutions—politically and theologically informed judgment would have devised a more useful and less divisive instrument.

It is worth noting that the only other major denomination which has undertaken the task of writing a contemporary confession is the Presbyterian Church in the U.S. The other denominations did not feel that their confessional standards were necessarily inadequate or antiquated. The Methodists reratify theirs line by line every four years in their General Conferences, for instance. From this it cannot be assumed that other Protestants did any better job than the Presbyterians in facing direct theological issues. But they had a better chance because they had a longstanding theological tradition and unaltered theological vocabulary to work with.

A Developing Protest

To understand just how bad a politics it was, the political scene of the UPCUSA in the early and mid-sixties must be recalled. First, the denomination—already a union of the Presbyterian Church in the U.S.A. and the United Presbyterian Church of North America in 1958—was in negotiation with the Presbyterian Church in the U.S. (Southern) to study reunion. And both of these churches were actively involved in promising conversations regarding a grand uniting of major Protestant denominations. The conversations were called Consultations on Church Union (COCU). Overcoming "our scandalous divisions," as Dr. Eugene Carson Blake called them in co-sponsoring the proposal for reunion with Bishop James Pike, was a theological bonus. The great immediate advantage of a COCU-style superchurch was seen to lie in the impact it could have on national affairs. An executive who represents something like forty million Protestant Christians can do a great deal of deliberate policy-influencing in Washington D.C.

Second, the UPCUSA in those days was so rich it didn't have to think about money. The Rev. Bryant George, now a Ford Foundation executive, once a Board of National Missions executive, said in the glory years, "The church could die and National Missions wouldn't notice the difference for five years." National Missions, along with the Board of Christian Education, and the Commission on Ecumenical Mission and Relations had reserve funds to fall back on—in case. The case in those days never arose. The General Mission budget of the General Assembly grew each year, and local Presbyterians increased their gifts accordingly. The three program boards used their reserve funds to support programs above the budgeted limits. In 1965 Presbyterians gave $39 million to the General Assembly General Mission effort, a trifle compared to the $317 million which church members put into the offering plates at the source.[12]

The success of "The Fifty Million Fund" indicates the solid healthy state of the denomination's economy. In 1964 a proposal for a capital funds drive was launched. The fund goal was an audacious $50 million. It was oversubscribed by $5 million.

Third, the denomination was organized in such a way that the annual meetings of the General Assembly had an overpowering importance for the whole church. The General Assembly was the national United Presbyterian church, and it appointed three high-powered boards to carry out its programs and policies. Furthermore, the boards had high-powered staffs, one of whose responsibilities was to make program and policy proposals to the General Assembly.

Although the 850 or so commissioners were elected by the 188 presbyteries and came from all kinds of different local circumstances, when they were convened into a General Assembly, they inevitably responded to an ambience of supercharged church statesmanship with consistently liberal enthusiasm. Conservatives didn't have a chance. With them it was 0–50 every year.

The ability of the board staffs to manipulate the General Assembly has in recent times grown in unchecked historical imagination trying to remember a conspiracy into existence.[13] The board staffs did exert a formidable pressure on every General Assembly. What the conspiracy-hunters conveniently forget is that the General Assemblies between 1959 and 1965 didn't require manipulation, or often a nudge. A big majority of commissioners came to the assembly ready to go—sometimes ahead of the staff people.

Fourth, there was a reorganization effort underway. A Special

Committee on Regional Synods and Church Administration had been appointed in 1963 to investigate overhauling the place of ungainly but basically useless synods in the UPCUSA organization. There were then thirty-five synods, generally conforming to the boundaries of a state, such as, the Synod of Pennsylvania. Synods were little more than annual meetings of delegates from presbyteries at which General Assembly program was explained, songs were sung, and speeches made. Synods were as useful—in Jack Garner's estimate of the vice-presidency—as a bucket of warm spit. The special committee wanted to revise the synod boundary map so that there would be maybe fifteen to twenty synods. Then the committee wanted to invest the synod with some actual power.

Behind this intention were two veteran ecclesiastical experts: the Rev. William Schram, a former executive in the Board of Christian Education and at that time pastor of the prestigious Hugenout Memorial Church in Pelham, New York, and the Rev. David Ramage, then an executive in the Board of National Missions, and now the executive director of the New World Foundation. Schram was the chairman, and Ramage was the staff man. They started out being most interested in creating metropolitan synods, like the Synod of Metropolitan New York City, or the Synod of Greater Chicago. It was a bold move to reverse the priorities of "an essentially anti-urban denomination" in order to get the power and the funds to mount a really effective urban mission. Ramage was an expert on urban mission. "We've got to be appropriately sophisticated about radical evil," he said.[14]

Fortuitously, the special committee put up its trial balloon at the Columbus General Assembly in 1965—the same year the draft of the brief statement was offered. The committee's proposal, offered for study and response, aimed to get the brand new power for regional synods from the powers vested in the presbyteries, which had always been the basic and characteristic Presbyterian unit. Despite their realization that the proposal would be mildly controversial, they offered it without a tremor of anticipation. They thought it would get refined and then pass. (It was not only shot down, it was demolished.)

Fifth, the Brief Statement of Contemporary Faith was offered in draft form at Columbus with overweening confidence. It was the party line of the liberal establishment, conceding for the moment there was one. The draft of the brief statement supported and even moved the policy framework of the denomination ahead somewhat. The fifteen members of the committee could not conceive the over-turn of the effortless liberal hegemony of the church. The politics of the brief statement is of a piece with the reigning politics of the day. It was a short-sighted and bad politics.

All along there had been greater resistance to the activities of the national church—meaning the General Assembly and its agencies—than a representative form of church government would force church leaders to acknowledge. They conceived their responsibility to be one of educating and leading your average angry Presbyterian to some better understanding of the gospel and its relationship with the modern world. They conceived their responsibility to Presbytery delegates and General Assembly commissioners in these terms: to present them with the opportunity to lead the denomination. The farthest thing from the leaders' minds was to believe they had a responsibility to *reflect* the views of the members. They believed their responsibility was to God, not to the members of the church. Therefore, the resistance of some alleged greater strength than met the eye at General Assembly was for church leaders an irritation. According to Paul J. Cupp, one-time president of the Presbyterian Lay Committee:[15]

> Back in 1963, there began some communication between a small group of United Presbyterian laymen in the Greater New York area and the top leadership of our church, expressing concern over the increasing empha-sis of the church in purely secular matters, and the evident neglect of the church's primary mission. These concerns were on several occasions ex-pressed in writing—and face to face—with strong convictions, to our church's leaders. The response of the church leadership in essence was this—whoever does not agree with the policies and programs of the United Presbyterian Church is free to go wherever he chooses.

I tend to credit this as an accurate reminiscence. That would have been the response of some top leaders all right, although I can't imagine their not having invited these conservative business persons to move on into the twentieth century as the happiest solution to their problem, and Cupp doesn't report their having made such an invitation.

There were indeed a lot of unhappy people in the UPCUSA. Before C-67 they were sort of unconnected and privately fed up. In the Presbytery of Chicago, for instance, a conservative pastor, the

Rev. Roland Showalter, said, "If you took a head count of every Presbyterian in the Presbytery, you would find a clear majority dissatisfied with the liberal policies of the national church and Presbytery staff, yet at Presbytery meetings we (conservatives) are outmaneuvered and outvoted every time. You would never know we are the majority." He was right but wrong too. He was right about the discontent a head count would probably have shown but wrong about its homogeneity; it wasn't *all* dissatisfaction "over liberal policies."[16]

The business of coming to dependable judgments about the quality and size of the existing discontent in the denomination before C-67, and as it was being debated, has been made much more difficult because since then Dean Kelley has written an enormously popular and influential book which seems to *settle* the matter. He has pressed an argument in *Why Conservative Churches Are Growing* that is ingenuously clear. We come to the difficulty of this business in any case by way of Dean Kelley's reigning explanation.

He reaches for hard data in the basic statistics of church membership, plotted from 1960 to 1970.[17] A drop-off is noted beginning in 1965, which gets steeper as it approaches 1970. Kelley argues that this has got to be the irreducibly basic indicator. If a church is growing, it is obviously in good shape. But if it stands still, it is not in good shape because it will immediately begin to shrink—which shows the members don't like the church. Factually, the church is its membership. In order to show that the UPCUSA decline can't be accounted for as some sort of general American apathy toward religion, he points to the meteoric rise in the memberships of the so-called conservative churches—the Mormons, Jehovah's Witnesses, Southern Baptists, and so on.

All that can *safely* be inferred from the UPCUSA statistics is the concrete size of the membership drop: 200,000 in five years beginning with 3.3 million members. Nothing else can be construed from the statistics, especially nothing can be made of their comparison with Jehovah's Witnesses merely because both groups are religious. The statistics of a growing church do not explain the statistics of a shrinking church. But Dean Kelley thinks a comparison is valid, furthermore that it provides a clue for understanding the decline in mainline churches. The so-called conservative churches understand that they are religious organizations and so attend to religion. That they are on the right track is attested to by the numbers of fresh converts in their ranks. The mainline churches have not attended to religion solely. And there is the source of the membership loss and discontent, Kelley thinks.

> The churches in their present plight cannot look to their membership for disciplined adherence to any particular role or meaning, so they are drawn to another option: to proclaim the meaning which the faithful *ought* to see in the social situation, to define the situation in such a way that the membership will recognize their duty and do it, to lift up a lofty standard in the hope that members will rally around it. That is the option which many church leaders have chosen today, but it has not worked out quite as intended. Instead of rallying the faithful around the flag, these leaders have found themselves at a greater and greater distance from their ostensible followers, waving the flag more frantically as the gap has widened. Thus the leadership has far outrun the followership, and not necessarily to the discredit of either, but to the loss of both. The situation is a by-product of the general attenuation of meaning in the major churches: the leaders—despite some valiant efforts—have not succeeded in making clear how the social action they invoke fits in with—in fact is required by —the meaning-system of the church.[18]

Kelley goes on to advise church leaders either to make the relation of the "meaning-system" to social action absolutely clear and demand social action (or else) *or* "throw in the sponge and settle for being a promiscuous social club."[19] There is the giveaway. He thinks that is what mainline churches are or are becoming, their promiscuity most accurately pictured in trying to provide "technological" social services[20] rather than the more distinctive and badly needed religious service they should provide—if they want to grow.

This argument concludes that the mainline churches did not meet the pressing religious needs of their memberships, probably had not for some time before the final evidence began to appear on the total membership graph in 1965. The mainline churches, instead, were flailing around in social action. This is somehow a function of not flailing around in religion. Therefore we could expect to have discovered in the head count Roland Showalter suggested, a thirst for religious experience unslaked by civil rights marches. This was the discontent. Dean Kelley may be right about other mainline churches, but his speculations about "meaning-systems," "flag waving," "leaders too far ahead of followers," mounted on top of the thin ice of uncomparable statistics, do not add up to a dependable or necessarily cogent explanation.[21]

Why people were unhappy and how many of them were unhappy are not matters which can ever be established for the basic and unchangeable reason that in every instance unhappiness is a personal matter. It does not disclose itself to any old statistic-hunter. Robert Townsend, with his flair for getting to the point, says, "That door is locked from the inside."[22]

The contours of the debate provoked by the draft document of the brief statement provide the only dependable evidence about the discontent, and at that can't be trusted 100 percent. The reason is too simple to mention, almost, but it is *the* reason, believe it or not. *Most ordinary, local, unleaderly Presbyterians didn't know anything about the document and wouldn't have particularly cared had they known.* Why overlook such a simple situation? The controversy developed among pastors and the clericalized laity, that is, elders who go to presbytery meetings, and elders who are elected as commissioners to General Assembly. They come to know almost as much as pastors about the political ins and outs of the denomination and become pretty fair amateur theologians in the bargain. This is an amazingly little-pondered fact. There were, for instance, 90,084 ordained elders in 1965.[23] That is the outside absolute number of lay persons who could have participated in presbytery, synod, or General Assembly debate. There were 12,874 ministers. Even if every one of the ministers and elders of the denomination got into the controversy, we would still be describing only 3 percent of the total denomination. Of course, only a small fraction of the 3 percent were actually interested enough to controvert. I am perfectly convinced that over 75 percent of the denomination wouldn't have been prepared to answer a simple question about the *existence* of the proposed C-67.

The controversy concerned very few, but it concerned them in unprecedented ways. There was something in the air, some bracing new populist enthusiasm. Local Presbyterians, both clergy and laity, began to understand themselves as "church leaders" on an equal footing with the "top leadership." The very *idea* of a distinction became irritating. A "top leadership" connoted ugly "elitism," and the "elitism" seemed to be something more than a vague paranoid sinisterism; it seemed to be lying right out in the open, *exposed,* in the draft document. Yes, they were being given an opportunity to discuss and refine the document before finally considering it for actual adoption as a confession, but too late. The basic decision (about reconciliation) had already been made and couldn't have been undone without starting all over again with a clean sheet of paper. What could be more "elitist" than that? They were being presented with a fait accompli.

Add that sort of resentment to the natural antagonism that surfaced around the "Reconciliation in Society" section, and something like the actual upheaval can be imagined. Unintentionally but quite specifically the political manner of the draft document brought together two strands of previously unconnected discontent: discontent over top leadership as such and discontent over the aggressive social involvement favored by top leadership.

Beyond this coalition, the draft document was the occasion for the formation of the Presbyterian Lay Committee. On December 1, 1965, "A Call to Presbyterian Laymen" was released in New York by an insurance executive and Presbyterian elder named Roger Hull. He called for the formation of a Presbyterian Lay Committee. Here is part of what he said:

> The work of this Committee will be carried on *inside* the church and within the existing organization of the church. It will not function as an outside group seeking to change or in any way oppose the stated religious purpose and tenets of the United Presbyterian Church. Rather, it seeks to arouse lay members to the need for more active Christian witness right in their own churches and communities, instead of having official groups of the church obscure the basic mission by appearing to speak for the whole church in pronouncements on such issues as rent control, slum clearance, the war in Vietnam, the support of any one political candidate, federal aid to education, mass transportation, and other issues in the lives of believers.[24]

Well, it turns out this sort of unfocused grousing had been going on for some time without ending in the formation of a new organization. C-67 did that. Paul J. Cupp recollects:

> Late in 1965, the first draft proposal of what was to become the Confession of 1967 was released. To many, its thrust was clear and alarming. There were many defects that disclosed what appeared to be an intent of the authors of C-67 to lay the basis for more open thrust into secular matters in which the corporate church does not have competence. The premise adopted was that every issue of life is essentially moral and spiritual and that all barriers are thereby removed against ecclesiastical intrusion. As you may remember, there was quite a furor, and another Committee was appointed to revise the statement. We became aware of the intent to include C-67 in a Book of Confessions and place it alongside

the Westminster Confession. . . . All of this, including some of the strangely all-inclusive interpretations based on the concept of reconciliation, gave the Lay Committee founders real warning of what was to come, and they determined to sponsor a viable organization and effort.[25]

The Presbyterian Lay Committee fought (and is still fighting) C-67 on a deliberately theological ground. Cupp contrasts redemption with reconcilation. "Redemption," he says, "highlights the importance of freedom while reconciliation implies the patching up of a dispute between two quarreling persons or nations or races. Redemption goes deeper. It aims to ransom man from intolerable conditions that have dehumanized him and bound his spirit. Reconciliation implies co-existence but not necessarily social justice. Redemption in Christ implies liberation without which there can be no social justice. This distinction between the evangelism implicit in the Great Commission and the social gospel is at the heart of our difference with our church leadership."[26]

Such a point merely shows that redemption can swallow up the content of reconciliation just as easily as reconciliation can swallow up the content of redemption—if either one is chosen as a dominant theological category. The better theological point, where C-67 is actually vulnerable, would be made about the wisdom or pertinence of gimmicky "catchword" sorts of themes and trends. But, obviously, redemption is no better than reconciliation at staving off inevitable trivialization.[27]

The other criticism of C-67—still being made—concerns its manifest political content. Conservative-evangelicals call the reconciliation of the confession a flat-out "secular humanism."[28] To the implicit claim of C-67 that every decent Presbyterian ought to be a liberal Democrat, conservative-evangelicals can say with as much justification that every decent Presbyterian ought to be a conservative Republican. And who is there to judge? Finally, the church judges, the very church the drafting committee represents, and the very church the conservative-evangelicals represent. And if debate is conducted on reconciliation as a blunt instrument to knock opponents' brains out with, the point of reconciliation has suddenly been lost. Where C-67 wanted to be strongest, it turned out to be a pushover. Critics have perceived that neither God nor even reconciliation was commissioning the church to mount these paraecclesiastical adventures into the social and economic life of the nation.

Church leaders were. The same church leaders who had been pushing little Presbyterians around for too long. And given the shape of the literal reconciliation decision, what could church leaders answer without incriminating themselves?

This was the bad politics of the reconciliation decision. Not that it provided the occasion for the formation of the conservative-evangelicals into an ongoing organization—which they would undoubtedly have done sooner or later—but provided them with a ready-made issue. They could legitimately debate the issues raised in the "Reconciliation in Society" section of the confession on extraneous grounds and never once have to display their natural economic royalism, superpatriotism, racism, or sexual fears. And while representing an actual minuscule portion of the church, the Presbyterian Lay Committee has taken on itself the happy task of standing up for all dissent in the church—and taking the credit for every new misery felt by church leaders. The bona fides of the committee are a sworn devotion to Jesus Christ and such extraordinary love of the UPCUSA that leaving would be unthinkable—or, well inside the permissible limits of church membership established by C-67.

The First Fruits of Trivialization

The protest, conceding for the moment that there was one or that whatever else it was it was also "the protest," was not created by the decision of the drafting committee to center C-67 around reconciliation. The placement of C-67's reconciliation almost as a metaphysical force between God and the church provided critical opportunity to attack the specific content of the confession legitimately—without reference to the issues it was raising. This produced the spectacular consequences. Had the issues of racism, civil religion, sexism, and economic justice been cleanly debated, the history of the denomination after 1965 would have been very different. But they were debated obliquely, recognized if at all out of the corner of the eye. What was always being debated was a big, powerful, and arrogant church establishment. That being the case, the center of decision-making about the establishment shifted from the General Assembly to the more provincial presbyteries, particular churches, chapters of the Presbyterian Lay Committee, and area consultations of the Special Committee on Regional Synods, where, you may be assured, enough alienation was being expressed to last reconciliation a lifetime.

Focusing attention on this so-called protest gains in substantiality what the movement did not historically have: real power or real organization. It was actually just a lot of random "bitching." The real power and the real organization belonged to the General Assembly and its agencies. Now, had the top management of the church been astutely Machiavellian, as they are now made out to be, they would have seen to it that the egghead C-67 got lost in the Revision Committee never to appear again. But they were bad politicians and saw to it that C-67 rolled into reality on schedule, barely revised and bristling with portended controversy. Once on the books as a confession with a theological authority equal to the Apostles' Creed and the Westminster Confession, its peculiar *linguistic legacy* went into effect. Courtesy of C-67 the hatchet people and stud hustlers of the church got a great set of new words—as a gift. The linguistic legacy began producing another series of consequences almost instantly. Given the changing denomination, reconciliation, or rather, the *mission* of reconciliation, became eligible for some pretty startling employment. You can't easily believe the way in which this basically innocent little reconciliation and the defenseless little mission of reconciliation were fallen upon and rendered limb from limb. "Mission of reconciliation" all by itself became the occasion for a process of trivialization that continues to this day. It is, for instance, the favored expression of the New Organization which assumed formal constitutional reality on January 1, 1973. In other words, there could have been no New Organization without it. See what it has come to mean:

The chief administrative officer of the New Organization was making a speech at the Louisville General Assembly in 1974. Toward the end of the speech he said:

> There are some who have said to me that the word *mission* has been too much overused; that its appearance in so many titles, indeed its appearance in the title of the name of the Council, that it has appeared in the formation of presbytery mission councils, and congregational mission

statements, that the use of the word mission grows tiresome. (Pause.) I want this morning to respectfully disagree with that. Because the church, if we are to be the church of Jesus Christ, we must be involved, we must be engaged and immersed in mission. To be so is not our option.[29]

During the dramatic pause there was an audible and widespread groan. It was an expression of frustration from Presbyterians who realized their top administrator, with four years to run on his contract, could not tell the difference between overuse and the near comical misuse of the term *mission*. (He resigned about a month later.) This totally typical performance stands near the end of the process of trivialization. Somewhere just past the middle of the process Professor Willard Heckel, freshly elected as the moderator (presiding officer) of the Denver General Assembly in 1972, typically proclaimed:

Let us make no mistake; reconciliation is not finding the lowest common denominator . . . but . . . letting every voice be heard. Let us leave this General Assembly in a spirit of love, not hate. Close votes and decisions must be made, but let us reach them in love.[30]

"Letting every voice be heard" is quite a ways from the risky, hostility-inviting action of the church in the world which C-67 calls reconciliation. But that is what the word had come to mean. It might also be noted that Heckel's kindly admonition fell as gasoline on a fire. The Denver Assembly was the most rancorous in recent history.

These very real linguistic consequences and the series of political consequences streaming from the reconciliation decision came together in the suddenly altogether different reorganization effort being superintended first by the Schram Committee and then by its successor, the Mason Committee. In time both committees made proposals aimed at a sweeping reorganization of the church so drastic that the UPCUSA was *newly* organized, not reorganized. The documents containing these proposals are widely available but for all their inestimable importance are practically unknown. There is a pity. They are so poorly written and so deadly boring that most Presbyterians wouldn't have the heart to read them carefully if they knew that the documents even existed. However, the documents should be read and pondered; they provide the clearest possible picture of trivialization, and especially of "the mission of reconciliation's" astonishing career. Curiosity no less than theological sanity proposes a careful, thoughtful reading of both documents.

In the first document reconciliation exists almost exclusively in an understood ellipsis following the word *mission,* or appears to exist there. One does not always know for certain. The Schram Committee made its proposals in a document entitled "Design for Mission." There you are. The old-fashioned mission, of mission*ary* fame? or the new-fashioned mission, as in urban mission, urged by David Ramage? Probably neither. The mission that document is a design for is the overall mission of the church—or, as C-67 would have it, the mission of reconciliation. Mission's first appearance in "Design for Mission" seems to bear out this possibility because mission seems to be an activity or a set of activities: "The Committee believes that the capacity of our church to be obedient to Christ depends to a significant degree upon effective organization for mission."[31] Mission may or may not depend on effective organization, but in this first appearance it is something the church does, and in order to do better attends to the institutional features of its organization. That mission is a shortened form of "the mission of reconciliation" becomes clear in this statement: "Under the Lordship of Jesus Christ, the church orders its life to express its corporate and dispersed nature and to be in mission to and for the world." But just this "being in mission" begins to sound suspiciously unlike having *a* mission or *the* mission—as a task or assignment for which the appropriate verb is *to do.* Being in mission might mean being in readiness to do mission, but if so, it is an awkward and misleading way to put the matter. The direct evidence seems rather to suggest that the unexplained omission of an article in the expressions *for mission* or *being in mission* indicates that a transformation of mission has occurred, from a task God has given the church to do into a characteristic of the church's being.

C-67 tends to present the church as a pure doing—of reconciliation. Forget the aim of the doing and concentrate on the pure doing, then by a great leap, the "of reconciliation" can be relegated into an ellipsis so that it is always understood, when convenience will call it into remembrance, as being what the church is all about, and thereby making the doing of the church—whatever it does—the doing of reconciliation: by definition. In this way mission becomes equivalent to what the church does and is the sum of everything the church does: by definition. The old demon if/then is loose again. If the church is defined as doing the mission of reconciliation, then the church's doing is reconciliation: by definition.

This is more than a casual shift in emphasis. It is breaking new theological ground. I suspect the reason can be found in the first three (of seven) "goals and objectives of the proposal in relation to church administration":

1. To define each judiciary[32] as an instrument of mission so that the church may perform its various God-given responsibilities.
2. To design each judiciary for mission so that all its efforts are focused on fulfilling its mandate.
3. To distribute the administration of mission so that it is assigned to the lowest judiciary that can most efficiently and effectively accomplish it.

While mission (without any article) is now a property of being the church and resides in the church normatively as something like a nature, there is some administration-mission work to be done on the job of defining the various judicatories as instruments of mission, and designing them for mission, then finally assigning the administration of mission to the lowest, most local, judiciary that can handle it. It is a mere administrative task of mission. The various judicatories are already instruments of mission. Whatever they do must be mission, accordingly, and whatever administration does to get them into good mission shape is mission too.

The report of the Mason Committee makes this point openly. "The C-67 recognizes the important connection between administrative renewal and renewal of the church," it claims,[33] then quotes from the confession directly:

Every order must be open to such reformation as may be required to make it a more effective instrument of the mission of reconciliation.

In such fashion does the confession's "reformation" become the committee's "renewal," but a mandate, more or less, to be in mission, defined in these apparently precise terms:

Definition of mission: The root idea of the word is "to send" and it declares in one word the purpose of the church which Christ calls to himself and sends to the world. This mission has been set forth in our Form of Government under the heading of the "Great Ends of the Church" (G.III.4). It involves the proclamation of the gospel for the salvation of men in worship, nurture, witness, and service, through word and deed appropriate and meaningful in contemporary society, with particular focus at the points of greatest human need.

And since the Form of Government has been cited, the section on the Great Ends of the Church had better be considered, recognizing what just happened to "reformation."

> The great ends of the church are the proclamation of the gospel for the salvation of men; the shelter, nurture, and spiritual fellowship of the children of God; the maintenance of divine worship; the preservation of the truth; the promotion of social righteousness; the exhibition of the kingdom of heaven to the world.

It certainly comes as an astonishment to find these "ends" of the church called its mission. In its prereorganizational setting mission was clearly and *always* related to the church's God-given responsibilities for doing something outside the church. "The proclamation of the gospel" qualifies in the antique view as a definite mission; so does "the exhibition of the kingdom of heaven to the world." Maybe, by stretching the point, "the preservation of the truth" and "the promotion of social righteousness" could get by as a mission, but only in advanced theological contexts. Here is what couldn't *ever* get by as mission: "the shelter, nurture, and spiritual fellowship of the children of God" and "the maintenance of divine worship." Before words could be squeezed around into different shapes, the church had a clear idea (a wrong idea perhaps but wrong for other reasons) that holding church services in Chillicothe, Ohio, and sending missionary doctors to India were very different activities. In that old view the church services in Chillicothe, Ohio, weren't much good unless the worshipers anted up the money to pay for the mission of the church being conducted in India.

It turns out the Mason Committee was most particularly interested in getting these very two great ends rebaptized as true certified mission, on a par with everything else the church also does. When it consequently appears that a set of nifty new robes for the junior choir must be balanced against a gift to some program for the self-development of peoples and a local church accepts its God-given responsibility to buy those new choir robes, well, it doesn't make any difference because the choices exist as equals in a clear theological continuum. The choir robes are the church in mission.

The reorganizers didn't want to say that all of the social involvements of the church are unwarranted. They are *also* a definite part of the church's job. The reorganizers wanted to identify the something else as mission, more in line with the sentiments of the protest, that wasn't social involvement. There is evangelism and Sunday school too. (When the Schram Committee ventured out into the denomination for area consultations on its 1965 proposal, the people at the apparent grass roots were saying things like, "All I hear in this church is Negro, Negro, Negro, and what I want to hear is Christ, Christ, Christ," and "We're tired of being told we're not good Christians because we don't parade with King. We're good Christians right here, reading the word of God and practicing what we preach."[34] The people were also telling the Schram Committee to leave the presbyteries alone and concentrate on tearing down the national boards like it was supposed to.[35])

The eventual point of all the labored fussing around with mission was to provide *confessional* legitimacy for the full variety of opinions and activities in the denomination. The way the committees seized on mission as a characteristic of the church's being is indicative of the need they felt. The deep and angry division in the church thus could be seen as no division at all but two sides of church life: social action and evangelism. There are prophets and there are priests. There are times for frantic action and times for reflective calm. There are times for the expenditure of resources and there are times for the gathering of resources. Of course there are differences of opinion and that is what reconciliation is for. Both committees noted Christ's command regarding "unity in diversity." They seemed pleased at his wisdom.

These are the first fruits of trivialization. *Mission,* as in the mission of reconciliation, is a fairly well-grounded term in C-67. This isolated term is gingerly lifted out of its linguistic context where it is grounded in a network of associated terms, then set down in another context. It does actually become a different term in the different context, but since it is spelled the exact same way, it seems to be the identical term. There is no compelling reason why the authors of the two reorganizational documents should not use *mission* and define it any old way they choose to. They didn't, however, do that. They used *mission* as though it were the same *mission* as the one in C-67, because in a trivial way it is.[36]

Were it not ingenuous, trivialization could be called manipulation, or advertising, or a number of other things. But the apparently guileless misuse of language contrasts trivialization with deliberate and calculative efforts to deceive readers. Trivialization can be recognized as a certain deafness to nuance, a certain rigidity in the obsessively rational movement of thought from A to B to C as though because there is movement it is a logical movement. Both the enthusiasm and certainty of theoremlike statements give them away.

The materials already cited show trivialization at work, and occasionally I have mentioned alleged possible reasons. The reasons are the drive mechanism of trivialization, which in every attempt to hide them become more eloquent. Behind the rational flat prose of the reorganization documents the enthusiasm of true believers in a certain definite kind of reorganization can be felt. For political and other dynamic reasons we are just now trying to understand, the reorganization committees saw something had to be done about the agencies of the General Assembly and the administrative structures they were supporting in the presbyteries and synods. These reasons naturally are never discussed in the reorganization documents. Rather than get into such a messy business, the two committees fasten onto the administrative-organizational details of a supposed national church malaise and, wouldn't you know it, propose administrative-organizational changes as the requirements of mission. It simply wasn't true. *This* was the reason: the reorganization effort had begun to assume a life of its own. It had become a "religious" activity alongside the denomination's religion. *It* had the "mission." The people involved in making the reorganization proposals were dedicated to installing a particular *kind* of organization, with a *particular* planning emphasis. They were not dummies, aimlessly fastening onto trivial details; they were card-carrying zealots. What gives trivialization its flavor, then, is not its rigid little-mindedness but its very purposiveness. Hence it is a mistake to assume that the reorganizers were passive reflectors of backlash demands. In taking on a life of its own, the reoganizational effort immediately transcended a mere backlash. These people had a *dream.*

The Global Significance of Brass Tacks

We need to be very specific. Other denominations have cleaned up their national staff organizations without making it into a global issue. The Episcopalians, for instance, tightened up interboard and intraboard relations from the inside, merely because it looked like a sensible and worthwhile thing to do. Organizational structure certainly was never dressed up in the grandiose clothes of a huge problem. The "Design for Mission," however, presents mere administrative overhaul as *the* global issue. In its preface to the "Design for Mission" the committee seems to admit that "organizational effectiveness is not the solution to the church's problems"—which would be a fittingly modest disclaimer to make were the problems which organizational effectiveness cannot solve described or even named. But they aren't mentioned. This is a tantalizing omission, the more so as the committee gets down to the brass tacks of the problems which organizational effectiveness can solve.

> When synod-presybtery boundaries fragment metropolitan areas, they become an impediment to mission. When the lines of administrative responsibility are overlaping and confused, they impede the church. When the administrative organizations of the church lack an effective relationship to the judicatory responsible for policy development and review, they create misunderstanding between the presbyters and administrators. When the church lacks effective and efficient channels for the development of a comprehensive mission strategy and a system of priorities for the allocation of resources, it is ineffective in its management of mission. When there is ambiguity about the role, responsibilities, and authority of administrative staff, there develop unnecessary tensions that hinder the creation of an interdependent team for ministry. When congregation, presbytery, synod, and General Assembly budgets are developed without prior definition of the highest mission priorities, there is a poor stewardship of the resources of the church.

These are brass tacks all right. Every one of the problems submits easily to a solution proposed by technical-organizational reason. And every one of the problems on the list is shown to have absolutely premiere importance as a pressing church problem. Although the problems are located in the administrative area, the urgency of their solution is located in the area of the church's faith, its mission, its being as a church. That is how brass tacks achieve global significance. The need for reorganization is administrative fuzziness; the problem is unresponsive administration; the answer is administrative clarity, provided by Christian faith itself. A very specific analysis of any one of the problems shows that Christian faith isn't involved at all. But another kind of faith is: the faith of true believers in one particular kind of organizational model.

28

Consider one of these problems in detail. "When the church lacks effective and efficient channels for the development of a comprehensive mission strategy and a system of priorities for the allocation of resources, it is ineffective in the management of its mission." Read as a statement of an existing problem, the statement is remote; moreover, it doesn't make much sense. There existed no *organizational* impediment to thinking and planning together across organizational boundaries. The available channels were telephones, the U.S. Postal Service, Western Union, or, in case of urgent need for face-to-face development, the airlines. The character of organizational relationships was not holding back this thinking together and planning ahead, but of course that is the point. The "Design for Mission" is not talking about mere thinking together and planning ahead. The exact and precious language is "comprehensive mission strategy . . . system of priorities . . . management of mission." Obviously the church does not have these items because it is just now hearing about them for the first time. To posit their lack as a problem is fairly unusual.

Read quickly, the exact and precious language appears to be just ordinary bureaucratic clumsiness, but these terms meant something very specific to the proposers. And when later it dawns on everybody else that "comprehensive mission strategy" is going to become a tediously churchwide planning process, managed by a corps of planning experts, and the new religious emphasis is going to be on doing the planning right—the new mission—the planning experts can triumphantly point back to the "Design for Mission" and behind that to C-67: "It's right there, man. That's what you voted for." "Man" will likely not answer, his eyes glazing.

Consider another problem on the list: "When synod-presbytery boundaries fragment metropolitan areas, they become an impediment to mission." The proposers focus attention on the problem of boundaries. The number one metropolitan area is Greater New York, stretching from mid-New Jersey all the way to Connecticut. Three synods and six presbyteries had responsibility for pieces of this area. Naturally there was a lot of overlap and acting at cross purposes. Historically, this very situation initiated reorganization in 1963. But in the rush for reorganization the inspiration for metropolitan synods (being "appropriately sophisticated about radical evil") got twisted out of its sockets. The problem had never been the boundaries themselves but the lack of willingness of Presbyterians to provide the massive resources necessary to conduct a metropolitan ministry.

All urban churches in a metropolitan area do not have the resources to deal with public education, housing, transportation systems, political machines, police brutality, welfare reform, narcotics abuse, political corruption, mugging, raping, juvenile violence, and many another urban problem. And until this writing the UPCUSA has never come close to conducting an authentic and comprehensive urban ministry anywhere. Fastening onto the problem of boundaries can be seen as a strictly trivial consideration of metropolitan situations, though vital to the success of the reorganization scheme—those regional synods. Fixing up the boundary situation, looked at soberly, will not necessarily produce either Presbyterian willingness or Presbyterian cash. In fact, with decision-making once lodged at General Assembly level shifted down one notch toward the people, those very anti-urban people who successfully resist effective urban ministry will exercise their anti-urban bias much more significantly. Real possibilities for an actual full-blown metropolitan ministry are reduced by unfragmenting the boundaries, which, it appears, the proposers didn't consider a serious matter. Neither did the vast majority of Presbyterians.

Here is something they all can appreciate as a serious matter: money. The proposers put the money problem this way: "When congregation, presbytery, synod, and General Assembly budgets are developed without prior definition of the highest mission priorities, there is a poor stewardship of the resources of the church." On its face this statement is a judgment on budget-making practices. None of the budget makers are thinking about priorities, therefore haven't defined the highest *mission* priorities, and as a result are guilty of poor stewardship. The remedy must lie in some other way of making budgets in which highest mission priorities are defined before the budget is written out.

There is a problem here all right. Being political by nature, budgets reflect the persuasiveness of special pleaders and particular interest groups. The one thing budget making absolutely is not is rational. Presbyterians do not start from the top with a clean sheet. In practice they begin with last year's budget and figure from there. People who want something in the budget try to get it in; people who want something to stay in try to keep it in. The whole thing is toted up with an eye to what sort of money can be expected to come in. This is a reliable procedure which has the great blessing of common sense adorning it and may very well be poor stewardship also—a theological judgment, after all, which would be rather in the province of God and would probably concern amounts of money and not the procedure of making up budgets.

The reorganizers—in the name of participatory decision making —recommend another procedure, one that features a specific process of prior defining according to mission criteria. The absence of this process is producing all the poor stewardship. Well, what would be good about the recommended good stewardship? Presumably the fabled mission would be the uppermost consideration instead of regular old negotiation, tradition, lethargy, and expediency. But how is mission to be related to the proposed priority list? Not willy-nilly. Enter the budget-planning whizzes with a dandy four-stage process guaranteed to introduce rational order into the previous political chaos. Shortly they will explain something which seems to have been obscure, or at least ambiguous. It is that not *each* but a connection of *all* the four budget-making units comprise the secret of budget making. There must be an interlocked system from local church to General Assembly using the four-stage process. And there must be some transjudicatory (even trans-General Assembly) criteria established in order to determine how items are placed on the mission priority list.

It is not explained how the recommended process is better than the old; it is presupposed. Two clear consequences of the new recommended process are visible to the naked eye. Budget making itself is now going to cost money. The money to pay for the whizzes will no doubt come "off the top" and will never have to be itself validated as a mission priority. And, once rational planning procedures are introduced into budget making, rational planners, not regular old participatory decision-making folks, are everlastingly going to have the inside track in the procedures of slicing up the money. Such a plan does away with the disadvantages of democracy and installs the efficiency of a junta. That may be excessive. More carefully, it can surely be said that the planning-process managers are the new and highest priority mission item. Robert Townsend warns what will inevitably happen. The whizzes "borrow your watch to tell you what time it is and then walk off with it."[37]

The Plain Meaning of Accountability

Trivialization is a term I have used for the purposes of ethical analysis. The language of the "Design for Mission" has all the poise and polish of marshmellow. This is an esthetic judgment. Were it rigorously made, most all official church language would fall. When I call attention to its triviality, I am making an ethical point about its inattention to the plain meaning of words, its pretentious precision,[38] and its specious rationality. Plainly, whether ingenuous or not, the language of the "Design for Mission" is misleading. It had consequences more serious and long lasting than mere esthetic irritation. Commissioners at two successive General Assemblies voted for its proposals. They didn't really know all they were voting for, and they were helped not to know by the great-sounding themes of "decentralization of authority," "regionalization," "participatory decision-making," and "accountability." These were things the church wanted; the church must have been pleased to hear, then, that what it wanted was exactly identical to what God was calling it to do by way of reorganization.

In trivialization one little thing leads to another. We move from a sublimely isolated reconciliation to a more churchy dislocated mission to a sick church organization to a really sick, dislocated, isolated General Assembly agency administration: the subject of the Mason Committee report. In getting there the reorganizers were being submissive all along to protest pressure. I want to be clear in reemphasizing the usefulness of the protest pressure to the reorganization effort. The reorganizers could point to the pressure and contend they were being responsive to what the church wants. And maybe they were, but if they were, it was a clever and useful responsiveness. Much nearer the heart of their effort, they were being responsive to their "dream," their religiously fervid commitment to a "new kind of church organization."

When the committee presented its report to the Rochester General Assembly in 1971, they had some audio-visual aids on hand to help the commisssioners get the big picture. The most revealing slides contrasted a Model "T" Ford automobile with a jet age vehicle. They intended, with God's help, to get this church shaped up to do some real business.

Under the heading, "The Need for Reorganization" the committee writes, "The need for reorganization of the church's national-level agencies has been apparent to many. Criticism of the present structure—not of persons or units but of the structural system—has included such points as . . ."[39] and then follows the catalogue of criticism. Well, *where* is the need for reorganization? Is it in the criticism itself, or in the Nixonian "many" making the criticism, or in the national-level agencies? Does the need exist objectively in the agencies, or does the need exist in having to heed criticism of the national-level agencies? It is an important question which the Mason Committee typically blurred.

Four other denominations have extensively reorganized their national operations or are presently in the reorganizational process. The newest Episcopal reorganization has all the appearance of being a response of the new Presiding Bishop, John Allen, to conservative protest in the denomination. The national staff was getting heavy criticism. That is the exception. In the case of the three previous Episcopal reorganizations, the reorganization of the United Church of Christ, the Presbyterian Church in the U.S., and the centralizing moves of the Methodist Church, the pressure has come from the objective unwieldiness of existing organizational structures. The matter in no other instance, as I understand it, has been blurred.

It is clear that the Mason Committee couldn't locate the need to reorganize in the structures because it simply wasn't true, and the committee would have no assurance about the outcome. But then the committee couldn't openly admit that the entire expensive, church-wrenching process was merely a response to criticism—a fairly trivial procedure, it would seem. So it did the best it could. It blurred the distinction. Other denominations can learn from Presbyterian experience. Presbyterians can learn from themselves; who knows, they may soon be re-reorganizing. And what they can learn is to demand to know the exact location of where the pressure to reorganize is coming from. But, never mind; here is the criticism, comprising somehow a certified list of problems:

- A maze of interagency committees.
- A lack of an effective coordinating unit.
- A multiplicity of programs.

- Duplication of programs and supporting services.
- A perplexing variety of staff and promotional services.
- A growing list of proposed new agencies.
- A proliferation of General Assembly special committees and commissions.
- Inadequate systems of accountability.
- Less than optimum efficiency and economy in use of personnel or funds.

Or, pure institutional sloppiness, seen in wastefulness and inaccountability. Criticism of the wasteful sort of sloppiness is well understood. To the extent a dollar given to God is spent wastefully, it is not well spent. The need to trim the organization of its fat is automatically valid any time and requires no further comment, except to note that in the report such simple statement of need can't be found. Were the problem put that simply, commissioners might recognize that the General Assembly could order a full-scale trim job on the existing agencies. It is not so much that the existing agencies are wasteful, therefore, but wasteful in obdurate ways, so wasteful in fact that they've got to be replaced altogether.

Criticism of inaccountability is not well understood. "Inadequate systems of accountability" are the exact words, but nothing more. This is the more important part of the sloppiness. But what is it? In what ways did the committee—or some of those "many"—find the agencies not adequately accountable? There is a great hole in the report exactly where such an accounting of this non- or semi-accountability might be expected to be found. There is a bit of explanation later in the report on what *adequate* accountability is:

> In developing an effective system of accountability there are several elements and factors that need to be taken into account.
> A. Management tools
>   1. With the development of a uniform system of accounting which is in process, there will be in the denomination for the first time a basis for comparing the budgets of the various agencies.
>   2. Through the use of modern management techniques such as management by objectives, it is possible to develop a more orderly and rational means of evaluating an agency's progress and effectiveness in achieving its assigned task.
>   3. With a clearer division of responsibilities among the proposed new agencies and the avoidance of duplication, it should be simpler for the commissioners to know whom to hold accountable and for what.

With the exception of the third item, accountability as a problem rests in the domain of treasurers, bookkeepers, and accountants, but not in the domain of commissioners. It is a technical problem which financial reason can always solve, and if later, certainly now. The third item therefore looms the larger for being more than a technical item. The suggestion is clear that without the new system of accountability, using management-by-objectives techniques, commissioners do not know whom to hold accountable or for what. So the question fairly pops out. What don't commissioners know that prohibits them from holding "someone" responsible-accountable for "something"?

The lack of candor is almost comical. And so is the absurd and trivial judgment that the existing *system* of accountability was somehow inadequate. The committee could perhaps ignore the actual placement of this issue in the church, but surely no one else could. Accountability had been about the number one subject for Presbyterian conversation since 1969, a fact that Orly Mason himself would have been peculiarly aware of.

In 1969 the General Assembly met in San Antonio. Early in this assembly James Forman made a surprise speech, by now understood to be one of his "famous" speeches. He presented his Black Manifesto and belabored white racists in the UPCUSA until winded. As was his practice he presented a particular claim on this particular denomination. He demanded $50 million as the Presbyterian share of the reparations due the black people of America.

He spoke in time docketed to the General Council.[40] After his speech the General Council asked the assembly to give it the responsibility for making a response to Forman. The generally stricken commissioners were pleased to concur with the request. All right, the question became: "How did James Forman happen to address the General Assembly under General Council auspices?" The question was raised immediately by some of the enraged commissioners. The moderator of the General Council, Dr. John Coventry Smith, said that it was plain he was going to speak anyway; so the General Council had decided to provide an orderly context in which the address could be delivered and a response framed. That wasn't satisfactory. To *whom* was it plain Forman was going to speak anyway?

Here the matter goes off the tracks because it is not clear to whom it was plain. The facts are that the council had heard from Forman's organization's representatives, and from the Board of National Missions staff, and from the staff of the Council on Church and Race, and somehow had concluded that Forman would make a scene as he had just done in the Riverside Church in New York, and in the Board of National Missions' offices in New York. Very well, who from Forman's organization, who on the church's staffs had been advising the council? "Responsible representatives" had.

There is the issue of accountability—neat. The aim in trying to locate the actual church staff persons who knew Forman and his representatives, and who knew about Forman's intentions, was to get to the bottom of what had every appearance of being the most outlandish "elitist caper" yet. It was simply understood that the radicals on the staff had engineered the whole appearance of Forman. What made it worse was that it was legal. The General Council was accountable and had made its accounting. The unhappy commissioners were therefore in the same position as the police officer reported by Tom Wolfe to have been standing across the road helplessly, watching a gigantic party held by Ken Kesey's Merry Pranksters for the notorious Hell's Angels. The officer is reported to have said he couldn't arrest them. "They're not breaking any laws," he said. "Except every law known to God and man."[41]

Orly Mason is a business person from Chillicothe, Ohio. He was an at-large member of the council, regularly elected. When the council convened after the Forman appearance, he was among those who favored making no response at all to James Forman. They thought the council should apologize to the assembly for the address it had seemed to sponsor. Mason was in the minority, it turned out. As that was becoming clear, he announced he was going to resign from the council and quit the church. Then he left the meeting.

Something happened to change his mind. It could be called a paradigm of reconciliation. Shortly after, he was appointed chairman of the vital new restructuring committee and didn't resign from the council or quit the church. His threat to leave the church because he thought it had sold out to black racism was honored with the most influential appointment moderator George Sweazey made that year. Mason knew at firsthand that the system of accountability had worked beautifully in San Antonio. That is what made him angry enough to threaten to quit a church he professed to love greatly. Therefore, when his committee identified the system of accountability itself as the faulty item, the background for such a judgment was that the system could be abused by black zealots. It should not be thought surprising that the committee's proposals contain drastic changes in the General Council, its relationships with program agencies, and to the General Assembly itself. *Adequate* accountability does not mean, you may be assured, "Staff will hereafter make full accounting for its actions and had always better be certain that there is sound justification for its actions"—about what accountability means anywhere else. *Adequate* accountability means, "Don't do it at all ever again!"

Accountability functions in the report as a code word which means, "No more James Formans." Commissioners understood that well enough and were probably sympathetic to the reasons for not mentioning what accountability really means, but they paid a price. Clear and believable public discourse suffered another setback, which will continue to manifest itself as mistrust, frustration, and alienation as long as Presbyterians have public meetings—and speak at them. That is the smaller part of the price. The bigger part is the silence that follows repression as night follows day.

National staff freedom was an expendable item to the Mason Committee; it didn't care about that. It was fascinated with its "churchwide planning process": the trembling essence of trivialization.

II

Reconciliation at Work

The most influential person in the UPCUSA since 1971 has been Angela Yvonne Davis. And she isn't a member. Hardly. She is a declared, proud, and, she says,[42] happy member of the Communist Party. So she thinks the UPCUSA, like any other church, is a tool of capitalist oppression. The Council on Church and Race (COCAR) of the denomination didn't care what she thought of the church. To them she was a great black sister in bad trouble, and they donated $10,000 to her defense fund. When the general membership heard about the gift, a tremendous fight developed. She broke the church wide open without trying. She hadn't asked for any money and maybe hadn't known any Presbyterian money had been given. But superb Marxist dialectician that she is, she is bound to appreciate the irony now; she became the occasion for truth to break out in another, theological, language system. In the ecclesiastical order she might very well have been the mysterious agent of God (who doesn't exist in her language system) sent directly to the UPCUSA. If so, the God who rules and loves the church, according to all ancient theological authorities and the C-67, has now displayed a tendency toward caprice and black humor which theologians would do well to watch.

This intellectually suggestive possibility didn't much occur to Presbyterians, wrapped up as they were in the business of "participatory decision-making" and "churchwide planning process." It did, however, occur to one of the commissioners at the tempestuous assembly in Rochester. Rev. Douglas Gray wrote breathlessly to *Presbyterian Life* magazine upon returning home:

> We were a crowd of church people inflated with our own righteousness. And the Christ came from outside and confronted us. "Scribes, Pharisees, hypocrites, . . . blind guides . . ." That's what he said to us. That's the way he came at us through some outside the fold. [The ellipses are *Presbyterian Life*'s.][43]

Mr. Gray seems to have Angela Davis in mind as the agency through which the Christ upbraided the UPCUSA in a manner he made familiar during the early part of the first century when, it is reported,[44] he said the same sort of things to liberal Judaism. This is the only place I can discover in the public record which admits that Angela Davis's appearance in Presbyterian history was supervised by or at least approved by God.

The best of the theological reflection on the matter has her as the enemy Christ commands the church to love. A theological professor, Gordon Jackson, took that line. He too wrote to *Presbyterian Life:*

> Cutting to the heart of the matter, the real question is: Do I love Angela Davis? My Lord couldn't embarass me much more. He always gets to the theological question: Do you love the enemy? Do you love her as I have loved you when I died for you? . . . Had he only left it at friends or nice people or good people. But his had to be the test of radical love—the stranger, the alien, the one outside the gate, the enemy. Of course, if his were not that kind of love, I'd still be outside the gate. [The ellipsis is *Presbyterian Life*'s.][45]

To which John Bodo, a former teacher of religion and renowned San Francisco pastor, is reported by a religious journalist to have responded that the love-your-enemy emphasis is correct. "I do believe, however, that we are not expected to finance them."[46] Professor Jackson would consider that a flip answer to a serious theological-ethical question he has raised. As he sees it, the command to love your enemy is quintessential. You can't think Christian faith or church without it. That is his judgment. And this judgment was questioned by a clever pastor named William Hudnut in a general reprise of the Davis controversy he wrote some months later. He takes on the love-your-enemies question and comes to a different conclusion. The alternate question, at least on a par with the love your enemies question, can be put in this form: Is the gift to her in keeping with the church's mission? Hudnut admits that we must all work hard at transforming the human race into a human family, *but*.

> But the question is one of judgment. Where do we take our stand? Where do we apply our resources? How do we implement our mission? Here is a woman accused of complicity in murder and kidnapping. Why should she become our special charge? We have to make discriminate judgments in history. Christ asks us to be wise as serpents as well as innocent as doves. His gospel does not compel us to finance the cause of a person who has said, as Miss Davis has, "The only true path of liberation for black people is one that leads towards the complete overthrow of the capitalist class in this country." We live in a tough world where many demonic powers are working to tear things apart, to uproot and destroy. The New Testament teaches that love builds up, and Christians should work for things that edify. Is it not wiser to apply our resources to the support of those persons in our church and outside who are exercising responsible creative leadership in arriving at solutions to our problems, than to finance our own destruction, as it were, by contributing to the activity of radical militant negativists who have declared war on our society and are deliberately advocating and conspiring for its overthrow?[47]

This is scarcely an elevated discussion, but it was openly theological. People were looking at the COCAR action from the standpoint of ideas. It was the exception. Mostly the controversy was not carried on theologically. It was an ecclesiastical-organizational matter and discussed in those terms, which should not be thought surprising for people who voted so easily in favor of the "Design for Mission."

The news that COCAR had made a $10,000 grant to Angela Davis's defense fund hit the General Assembly like lightning. The news got out on Wednesday, May 19, and although the grant was not presented formally until the following Monday, and then not debated until the next night, it was the number one issue of the assembly. There was something about the manner of the grant which added to its already sensational character. COCAR approved the grant in February; the check was sent to the Office of Ethnic Church Affairs, a coordinating body of the Synod of the Golden Gate, in April. The executive of that office, Rev. Eugene Turner, hadn't actually turned the money over to the Davis defense fund until May 14, just before the assembly began. The recipient of the grant was thus listed as the "Marin County Defense Fund" in the papers provided commissioners assigned to the Assembly Standing Committee on COCAR. They asked what that meant and seemed to have discovered an artlessly buried Angela Davis. It had all the markings of a cover-up. The sick joke of the assembly was: "COCAR was caught red-handed."

Here are the elements of the puzzle: The St. Andrew's Church in Marin County issued a statement in December, 1970. It was a position paper on the prosecution of Angela Davis. These Presbyterians were worried that the state of California would use the occasion of her trial to break the back of the black struggle. The paper made no requests; it was an expression of definite and well-thought-out concerns.

Eugene Turner saw the statement and sent a copy to COCAR in New York, which, he knew, had a $100,000 Emergency Fund for Legal Aid. *Technically* he was transmitting a request for legal aid from a local church session,[48] although there was no explicit request for funds in the St. Andrew's statement. *Technically* the fact he made the transmission signifies a concurrence with the request, although he made no request either. *Technically* a grant to the Marin County Defense Fund was approvable because it met the guidelines of the emergency fund requiring it to come from lower judicatories through higher judicatories to COCAR.

For every technically, however, there were alternating technicallys. To wit: St. Andrew's had made no request; neither the Redwoods Presbytery officially, nor the Synod of the Golden Gate officially had seen the (non-)request and had not concurred with it. The whole thing came as a big shock to the members of these judicatories when they heard about it, along with everybody else. The most important alternating technically was this. *Technically* COCAR had made no effort to establish the need of the recipient, which the cold language of the emergency fund's guidelines specifically requires it to do.

So that is where the matter was at in the assembly, in the technically thicket. COCAR was rebutting as hard as it could and trying to represent itself as having been scrupulously faithful to the guidelines, when it was clearly as mean-minded and punctilliously legalistic as its critics. COCAR really had a better ecclesiastical-organizational case to make for itself than it ever made at the assembly. After being beaten atop the head with the Constitution, Bible, and "Design for Mission" for three months, it drafted an overall response in which it pointed to the language of its own institution, no less than to other crucial language in the institution of the emergency fund. Much, much too late COCAR wrote:

> The church cannot be bound only by the values and traditions of the majority. The challenge is to the church, in part through the ministry of those the General Assembly has elected to the Council on Church and Race, to continue to "comfort the afflicted and afflict the comfortable," to dare to champion unpopular causes if this is the will of Christ, and to immerse the church in the milieu and experience of despised, neglected, and oppressed peoples in order that we may "share his sufferings, becoming like him in his death, that if possible (we) may attain the resurrection from the dead." (Phil. 3.10–11) Faithfulness can mean no less.[49]

The denomination had set up COCAR precisely for the purpose of representing to a basically white church the needs of a black community it wouldn't know how to know much about. So COCAR had recognized Angela Davis's need—in a far more acute and expert way than white people could have—and responded, as it was supposed to do period. For the General Assembly to become overnight experts in black experience and overrule the experts it had elected is just about as close to racism as a racially liberated denomination can get.

I doubt that even this valid legal-technical point would have impressed the General Assembly, however, had COCAR thought of it in time. The debate was all about the propriety, the wisdom, the need, and the legality of the grant. Concretely the debate centered on an amendment offered by Rev. William A. Walmsley of San Jose, California; it directed "that the 183d General Assembly communicate to the Council on Church and Race (COCAR) its serious questions concerning the propriety of allocating $10,000 to the Marin County Black Defense Fund."[50]

The most important aspect of the debate historically was its interracial character. Out in the heartland of the denomination it would later prove easy for Presbyterians to tell themselves that black Americans can too get a fair trial without some fancy and expensive legal defense fund. But on the floor of the General Assembly there were black Presbyterians saying that COCAR had been absolutely right; Angela Davis wouldn't get a fair trial, they suspected, even with the greatest legal defense money could buy. The black presence added a touch of realism to proceedings whose true shape would emerge in the postassembly reaction, that is, in congregational and session meetings where there were not now and never had been any blacks.

The great issue was the simple one: Angela Davis was a Communist. The grant seemed to support her and therefore her communism. There was no debate on that issue. Everybody condemned her communism—and every other possible kind of communism. Probably the only thing the assembly was unanimous about the entire ten days was how much the UPCUSA hates communism. Advocates of the grant naturally lamented her political beliefs but argued they had nothing to do with her right to a fair trial. This infuriated opponents of the grant because they saw that her political beliefs were aimed at the destruction of the fair-trial system.

The architect of the amendment got around eventually to conceding the fair-trial issue. Probably she couldn't get a fair trial, *but.* "COCAR ha[s] not demonstrated to me that Angela Davis has this need of funds." The *Presbyterian Life* report, which I am following, goes on with a summary of his speech. "There are still many poor blacks, he said, who need legal defense, but lack publicity, support, and financial aid, all of which Angela has. He asked the Assembly not to do something that would divide the church; there are many needs—such as the problem of hunger—that can be met without 'rending and sundering' the church we love. Finally, he pointed out that his motion does not condemn the fund. It simply questions the propriety of the Davis grant."[51]

This argument has a spiral effect. It begins by challenging the alleged compassion of the grant. Walmsley makes a show of pointing to the *really* hungry, poor, and jailed colored people in this country —unknown, uncelebrated, undefended—who won't either get a fair trial. What about them? The basis for such a challenge is the assumption that the popular Angela Davis can get all the money she needs from her kind. But the challenge spirals into something else—a challenge of COCAR's procedures. Why didn't COCAR certify her concrete indigence? Thereby the warmth of concern used to begin the argument spirals into about the same quality as the concern of the welfare administrator smelling the ADC mother's breath in order to certify that she hasn't been misusing government funds on frivolous booze.

After two harsher amendments were beaten back, the vote was taken on the Walmsley amendment (raising the serious questions) and it passed, 347–303. It was a totally stunning defeat—unpredictable and unprecedented. But as the post-Assembly reaction began to come in, the closeness of the vote appeared to be a fluke. Out in the big middle of the church a different kind of vote was being cast, overwhelmingly against the grant.

The Great Offering Plate Boycott

Were we to revive existentialist ethics and conclude that the Presbyterians were guilty of bad faith, the judgment would be correct and beside the point. That the arguments against the grant were jingoist, racist, sexist, and decadent goes without saying.[52] But such a judgment has no feeling for the dynamics of this particular controversy when it occurred. It is more ethically central to the controversy to note its instant reduction from the size of global theological importance to the limits of a snit about guidelines, propriety, and other such ecclesiastical and turbid trivia. William Hudnut's elevation of the mission of the church into theological supremacy is now all the more revealing. He expressed the new consensus among Presbyterians. The "peace and unity of the church" became superior to its love and justice and thereafter would be the basis for grading love and justice.

The Stated Clerk of the General Assembly, William T. Thompson, himself a lawyer and a long-time civil libertarian, had tried to prevent the formation of this consensus. He wrote an elaborate defense of the grant in the July 15 edition of *Presbyterian Life.* He defended its legality, wisdom, courage, and, above all, its need. "The real test of whether the right to a fair trial by jury is available to all citizens is whether or not it is available to a citizen whom the vast majority of other citizens would decry," he wrote. "The rights of all citizens are assured only when the same rights are protected even for one who openly espouses a hated ideology and who is charged with a heinous crime." That is where he, chief executive officer of the General Assembly, lawyer, American, and individual Presbyterian stood. Then, as the stated clerk, he urged that "followers of Jesus should seek to love enemies and persons accused of capital offenses. The church is concerned about the equal administration of justice to a black woman because of the gospel of Jesus Christ." Then he

44

by-passed the degraded reconciliation of his own church's C-67 and quoted from a message to member churches from the Uniting General Council of the new World Alliance of Reformed Churches, which met in Nairobi, Kenya, in 1970:

> Reconciliation is the renewal of life based on God's word of judgment and forgiveness. It is the costly and joyous process of change, of personal and social conversion, in which God liberates us and enables us to move forward as hopeful people confident in his promises to make us fit instruments of his will.

And on *that* basis Thompson got to the heart of his own message to his own UPCUSA:

> Let us seek reconciliation, beginning with open acceptance of the sincerity and commitment of those with whom we disagree, and resolve to work within a church sufficiently inclusive of diversity to welcome us all.

His message was a total loss as far as reconciliation was concerned. Opponents of the grant wanted him to repudiate it. Proponents wanted him to blast away at its racist opponents. Reconciliation didn't touch them. They didn't change their minds, nor did Jesus Christ step in and change their minds. What did they care about some meeting in Nairobi? When it comes to the crunch, what did they care about reconciliation? It had already been used so many different ways, made into an item in a slide show, tossed around as though plastic putty, until it was something else mixed in with thrust, implement, planning, and those other no-words. And he was unable to prevent the formation of the new consensus.

The deepest suspicion of all begins to emerge at this point. The reconciliation decision of C-67 was intellectually wrong on its merits, not because of unpredictable and whimsical consequences which the drafting committee could neither foresee nor control. Reconciliation has no regard for the historically important social and political location of a fight, or enmity between human beings, or war. The ending of some fights on cue from a mistaken love for concord can be profoundly unjust. One can see the efforts of the authors of C-67 to overcome such an enormous objection by trying to relate the pattern of Jesus' life to the church's life. Maybe, they hoped, this will provide historical location.

> The life, death, resurrection, and promised coming of Jesus Christ has set the pattern for the church's mission. His life as a man involves the church

in the common life of men. His service to men commits the church to work for every form of human well-being. His sufferings make the church sensitive to all the sufferings of mankind so that it sees the face of Christ in the faces of men in every kind of need. His crucifixion discloses to the church God's judgment on man's inhumanity to man and the awful consequences of its own complicity in injustice. In the power of the risen Christ and the hope of his coming the church sees the promise of God's renewal of man's life in society and of God's victory over all wrong. The church follows this pattern in the form of its life and in the method of its action. So to live and serve is to confess Christ as Lord. (9.32,33.)

This is a brilliant and perhaps inspired effort, but doomed. The patterning is by nature a liturgical activity, hence inescapably religious, and hence will have a social and political location of its own. Radical feminist theologians have been devastating in their critique of the social-political location of the liturgy, for instance.[53] If conducted in a context of laissez-faire patriarchal male supremacy, they contend, the language of the liturgy has no leverage on the context. Jesus' "crucifixion discloses to the church God's judgment on man's inhumanity to man and the awful consequences of its own complicity in injustice," but in a vacant and abstract way. When concrete moral insight perceives that a considerable part of man's inhumanity to man is an inhumanity to women, the supremacist context smoothly and automatically invalidates the insight because that is not what the crucifixion discloses. Who says what it discloses and does not disclose? Well, men do, it seems.

The patterning of the church's life on Jesus' life is not safeguard enough against the corruption of justice which reconciliation is always dangerously near to. Furthermore, the patterning itself is subject to corrupting forces of socially and politically conditioned interpretation. C-67's valiant attempt to drag the innocent reconciliation into the places it is supposed to be related to ends poorly. As I say, it was doomed. Anything close to the liturgy is bluntly ecclesiastical-spiritual and therefore unprotected against the ravages of religious misunderstanding. Discerning the task of the church from the life of Jesus could come to an amiable split about whether Angela Davis is the enemy whom Christ wants us to love or a demonic power whom Christ wants us to battle.

C-67 had hoped to instruct the church about trouble spots in the world, such as the Davis grant seemed to be getting at. And it ended up being manipulated into the position of addressing the trouble spot of the church. Or, as Kurt Vonnegut, Jr., would say, reaching for the excruciating banality such an occasion demands: "So it goes . . ."

The intellectual credentials for the possibility that Angela Davis was the agent of a surprising and unpredictable God with a great sense of humor are numerous.[54] The leading one is that she came out of nowhere and was absolutely upsetting. Furthermore, she became a producer of consequences of such providential prodigality that they must be measured equal to the consequences of the reconciliation decision itself. You date things from her appearance. You see things in relation to her. She becomes a *factory* of consequences, which naturally began to conflow almost instantly with the forces alive in the rush toward reorganization. She changed those forces too. Whether with God's blessing or in spite of God's best efforts, Angela Davis left her mark on the UPCUSA.

Presbyterian Life went to press with its July 15 edition on July 8. It carried four full pages of letters in response to the COCAR action and the General Assembly's following action. The editors noted that many of the letters being printed had been abbreviated to avoid repetition, and that the letters printed were representative. The volume of response to the magazine, the stated clerk, to the moderator—Lois Stair—had been even in that short a time after the assembly "altogether without precedent."

The *Presbyterian Layman* was naturally ecstatic about this windfall of ill-will and added four full pages to its July issue in order to print the letters it had received and provide background information on the grant to its readers.

The Presbyterian Office of Information said in September that the communications to the officials of the church on the grant exceeded 10,000 and were critical of the grant overwhelmingly. According to *Presbyterian Outlook* the ratio was 70:1.[55]

The printed responses add little to the arguments made in the General Assembly debate. These points are regularly made in the letters available in the public record:

1. The grant was illegally made.
2. It was splitting the church, therefore should not have been made.
3. It implied a criticism of the American system of jurisprudence's capacity to provide Angela Davis with a fair trial without her fancy one-quarter of a million dollar defense fund.

4. It supported an enemy of religion and America.
5. Angela Davis didn't need money.
6. Lots of needy black defendants need the money more than she does.
7. It was a misuse of precious church dollars which could better have been spent elsewhere.
8. It was a shame.

The most revealing letter was printed in the *Presbyterian Layman,* which mentioned only that it came from a church in Kansas City, Missouri.

> Whereas, although we believe that Miss Davis, as a human being, is entitled to the love of all Christians, and as an American citizen, is entitled to the full protection of the American system of justice, nevertheless we have doubts as to the propriety of using the Legal Aid Fund in her defense, for the reasons . . .

The reasons are not unusual, but the preamble is. The opening conjunction *although* has the force of "in spite of the fact." At least that is what fair-minded grammarians would probably agree it means. This happens to be what the adverb *nevertheless* means, even when it is used later in the preamble as though it too were a conjunction. Strictly parsed, the second "in spite of the fact" cancels the first, just as a second negative negates the first or two minuses make a plus. But with the Communist terror loose, who is thinking about strict parsing? In this statement the two "in spite of the facts" reenforce each other in such a way as to produce the startling admission that in spite of the fact *squared* that "Miss Davis" should be loved by all Christians and should receive a fair trial as an American citizen, the Kansas City Presbyterians don't think the money should have been given to her. This blurts it out. *Were* the demands of the Christian gospel and the constitutional rights to a fair trial to obligate them to support the grant, they would repudiate both. That is the plain meaning of the statement, nowhere else made so boldly. They obviously think there are no such obligations.

Taken together the letters published in the various publications offer a student of religion a veritable gold mine of religious phenomena: disgust, rage, hatred, vengeance, ignorance, bigotry, lying—in fact, the only one of the Ten Commandments these letters do not break or contemplate breaking is the seventh, whose omission, by iron-clad Freudian laws governing repression, forces the postulation of some kind of lust out there among Presbyterians for this sensationally good-looking woman, thoughbeit Communist, black, and a professor.

The upshot of most of the letters from sessions was not the relief which comes from what popular psychological theorists call "ventilation." The upshot was an action. Here are some examples, which should be read in each case as though a long calendar of reasons had just been presented, that is, the actions stand on this side of some giant *therefore:*

> Our session has seriously considered holding in escrow our General Assembly contribution until this matter is settled. . . . If some satisfactory reconciliatory step is not taken by October 1, 1971, and announced to the Presbyterian Church membership at large that situations such as the Angela Davis incident will not be repeated in the future, our session and congregation will have to judge their 1972 contributions to the General Mission in that light.[56]

> This session will continue to designate specific purposes for all our contributions to the denomination, and will hereafter closely scrutinize any further gifts to the Synod . . . and Presbytery . . .[57]

> This session intends to pursue a policy of direct benevolence giving of the mission and benevolence funds of this church and further intends to withdraw and discontinue all benevolence pledges of any mission funds to the Presbyterian church under designated giving.[58]

> The treasurer of this church is directed to suspend forwarding further funds to the Central Receiving Agency pending a determination of future action. . . . A special committee . . . is hereby directed to make a study and prepare recommendations to the congregation on the following: A. Appropriate action concerning our mission giving in the remainder of 1971; B. Reconsideration of the previous decision concerning the allocation of excess funds received or to be received in 1971; and C. Designation of funds in 1972.[59]

> We declare to the citizens of our community, and to our own church membership, that we will designate all of the benevolence monies contributed to this church in a manner that is consistent with this declaration of dissent, with our historic confessional faith and with our respect for the integrity of the government of the U.S.A.[60]

> The session states that it will be its policy to re-orient its benevolence giving and emphasize specific projects over which it can exercise local control until such time as this session regains faith and confidence in the leadership of this denomination.[61]

Presbyterian budgets are usually set up in two sections. In one budget the expenses of the local church are treated: salaries, maintenance, soloists, office supplies, and so on. Then the benevolence budget treats the money going outside the local church to local, regional, and national causes. The biggest national cause normally is the General Mission of the General Assembly. This is usually the single largest item in the benevolence budget. That is what these sessions are talking about when they use the term *benevolence money.* They are going to restrict, cut back, put in escrow, or cease giving money to the national church. The portions of the letters cited all come from churches which felt comfortable having their names and resolutions printed in the *Presbyterian Layman,* that is, churches which would not be offended if called "conservative-evangelical." These letters do not therefore constitute a fair sample of the actual total action taken by all kinds of sessions, whether by formal resolution or just by doing it. Of the twelve hundred letters received by church officials, two hundred indicated that General Mission giving would be diverted in some way or other.

It was no less than the actualization of the "great offering-plate boycott," which had, before Angela Davis, been merely something to keep church bureaucrats awake nights worrying. After Angela Davis it was real and unmistakable. The proof is in the hard numbers which show that the bureaucrats had had reason to be worried. Taking 1965 as a baseline of normalcy—the way things used to be —there is a drop-off portending trouble from 1967 onward, getting ever steeper.[62]

	Total to GAGM	Total Receipts	Membership
1965	$30,999,669	$317,076,542	3,308,622
1966	30,946,605	330,035,826	3,298,683
1967	31,246,024	353,311,894	3,268,761
1968	29,945,599	349,732,687	3,229,724
1969	29,078,509	353,084,464	3,172,760
1970	27,250,431	357,829,446	3,095,791
1971	24,624,541	368,799,094	3,021,369
1972	22,597,440	373,211,983	2,916,567
1973	20,351,360	410,469,560	2,817,052

The big numbers first. The churches' General Mission giving dropped off 34 percent between January 1, 1965, and December 31, 1973. But at the same time total receipts—the gross money placed in the offering plates and spent for any and everything—rose almost 23 percent. Thus, had there been stability between ability to give and willingness to give, as there had been before 1965 when the two figures climbed impressively and at about the same rate each year, the General Mission giving would have been $38,130,000 in 1973, instead of the actual $20,351,000. *That* is the really big number, that difference.

It is clear that the biggest drop occurred in 1971—$2,626,000—but not sensationally bigger than 1970—$1,828,000—and both 1972 and 1973 where the drops preserved the 1971 drop and added over $2 million a year to it. The drop-off didn't begin in 1971, but it was in that fateful year that the already existing tendency to with-hold gifts to the General Mission was intensified and dramatized. Finally surfaced, it was a naked political effort calculated to punish the General Assembly agencies and force them to change policies.

As early as 1967 the Long Range Planning Committee of the General Council had identified an "alarming gap" between the positions of the "national church" on social-political issues and the positions of local Presbyterians. A special committee set up to look into the long-range financial future reported that the main reason for the drop in giving was "the lack of communication or understanding between those who plan the church's programs and those who are expected to support them." The committee said it had run into this reasoning time and time again. "Many reasons were given for this. Certainly the position the national church has taken on some social, political, and theological issues has been a factor in inhibiting giving."[63]

This old-fashioned enthusiasm for the restoration of communication between the national church and the local churches and the cultivation of mutual trust and respect, read now, seem almost touching—and absurdly naive. Already it was possible to see a native intuition at work in the churches that withholding money was the perfect way to force the agencies of the national church to change their policies. Communication had very little to do with it. The people in the local churches knew too well what the national church was up to and why, and they didn't like it. They didn't relish having their money spent on activities they disapproved of. They paid the bills, after all, so why shouldn't they have some control over how their money was being spent?

Eventually the substance of what the special committee did not see became widely and unmistakably visible. The stated clerk saw it in the first batch of reactions to the Angela Davis grant and started to head it off. He pointed to the unreasonableness of boycotting the whole General Mission program in order to express dissatisfaction with one council—which had *not*, he firmly pointed out, used General Mission funds in the Davis grant. The Emergency Fund for Legal Aid was composed of money which came out of the Board of National Missions' reserves, which fact made the boycott seem doubly unreasonable. He calmly pointed it all out:

> Withholding General Mission funds simply means that programs financed through them must be curtailed—programs such as hospitals, educational institutions, evangelistic efforts at home and abroad. Reduction of General Mission funds means that missionaries and fraternal workers cannot be sustained and ecumenical cooperation must be similarly cut back. Most of those who withhold funds because of the grant for the defense of Miss Davis will be distressed to learn the results of their action a year or two from now. If any number of them carry out their announced intentions, programs which these same persons approve and wish to advance will have to be cut back or abandoned.[64]

Thompson made a beautiful, extraneous point. His reasonable and thinly masked fury was the *point*. The boycotters didn't feature themselves as punishing the program. They were punishing the stated clerk and the whole national staff in the Interchurch Center, 475 Riverside Drive, New York City. *You*—all of you—gave us Angela Davis, so *you* must bear responsibility for any curtailment of program. You change the policy and apologize to the church and fire the loonies who pulled the scheme off and then we'll give again. It is up to you, for it is your fault not ours. One of the members of the Board of Directors of the Presbyterian Lay Committee made that very point: "Officialdom cannot properly lay the full burden of this situation in the laps of the givers. It must itself assume a very considerable portion of the blame."[65]

The New Organization Starts in the Red, Headed Downhill

The managers of the new organization which the Rochester General Assembly got on its way do not look upon the Angela Davis controversy with lighthearted theological wonder. It was a disaster and has plagued them every step of their way into the new era of good feeling that was supposed to have been the outcome of reorganization.

Because of the controversy, national giving was reduced. Rather than close down mission program, unrestricted reserve funds were used to make up budget deficits in 1971 and each year after. The reserves were substantial but nonetheless finite. In a presentation to the Louisville Assembly a bright and superrealist lawyer named Richard Miller, speaking for the 1975 General Mission budget, told the commissioners that the commitments made by past General Assemblies on the reserve funds had reached, in fact exceeded, the amount of existing reserve funds. As a consequence, deficit financing of the 1975 budget by use of reserve funds would be at least immoral and probably illegal. The 1975 budget would have to be determined in light of gifts alone, estimated to be no more than $26 million. But the sharp pencil experts from the agencies had brought in a minimum—rock-bottom type—budget, sized $32 plus million. Miller therefore advised the assembly and its agencies that a cut of 25 percent was required in order to stay within bounds of *legality*.

That's not the half of Richard Miller's bad news. The entire 25 percent cut would have to be sustained in the General Assembly level operation. And that disastrous reality has a story of its own. Early in the life of the new organization a decision had to be made about the (merely) desolating shortage of General Mission funds. This was in 1973, when the financial picture was only abysmal, that is, relative to 1974, relatively good. The policy decision was a naked bit of "participatory decision-making." Representatives of the regional synods shared the decision with General Assembly level representatives. An agreeable policy was determined. Priority was given to the formation of the new synod staffs and to the presbytery staffs requiring synod support. They were funded at 100 percent of their need; for awhile the national level staff of the new organization was to receive 65 percent of its formal stated needs. It was after all still locating and hiring staff according to intricate new personnel procedures. The new organization couldn't have filled all its slots anyway.

That policy decision was in force when Richard Miller relayed the bad news. The synods would continue getting their full 100 percent; the national operation would have to sustain the entire cut at about the exact moment it had gotten together its 65 percent full staff. This meant that some persons hired in 1973, freshly moved to New York, freshly leased, freshly mortgaged, freshly uprooted from somewhere else, would have to be terminated, not for incompetence or inefficiency or disloyalty, but simply and only because the folks who had hired them hadn't, well, looked far enough down the road. Since most of the fired staff happened also to be women and minority persons, they had a double beef; first, the suspicion of discrimination is heavy, and second, the suspicion of budgetary ineptitude is overwhelming. Did the sharp pencil experts not actually anticipate the reserve funds' exhaustion before it was pointed out to them? Put another way, if the church should be run as a modern, efficient business, is this any way to run a business?[66]

It might be argued that by its own reckonings the new organization should be neither happy nor sad with a budget of $26 million, $15 million, or $92 million. The budget—of whatever size—would represent a set of decisions made in accordance with the "churchwide planning process" it has installed. If that's what the church decides, the new organization has no occasion at all *in its theory* to worry about ecclesiastical facts, but that is in theory. In practice the budget whizzes felt comfortable in accepting the 100 percent–65 percent initial policy definition because they had stars in their eyes. They were inhaling the intoxicants of church leadership. They believed the worst of the crunch was over. General mission receipts would swing upward as the denomination began to see the fruits of a new era of trust and love and . . . and . . . In a word, they were disastrously mistaken. Instead of accepting the ecclesiastical facts as the given, they refused even to *look* at the facts. Of course. Beneath all the rational process talk of the new organization's managers, they are sad, angry, and perplexed. Things haven't worked out as they were expected to, thanks to Angela Davis, thanks to the boycott, thanks to letting the synods "rob" them blind, thanks to a lot of things.

It should be no surprise to discover the new organization was born into hard times it had no means to understand. When a church, in sharp distinction from a corporation or a government, begins to reorganize, four things generally can be assumed. 1. There is a fight which the reorganization is supposed to settle, dodge, or push off into obscurity. 2. A corps of experts will be hired to make proposals about the old organization. They will analyze it as an organization, and without reference to the fight. They therefore will find organizational defects and attempt to fix them. 3. After the proposed changes are made, the corps of experts will be running the newly organized church. 4. The fight will still be going on. Common sense makes these assumptions; experience teaches them. The proposers of the new organization used the fight to get their way. The new organization apparently believed its own PR, thus it thought that the whole unpleasantness would disappear as soon as the new order was in place.

Historically, the rush to reorganize and the crystallization of protest in a concrete budget reprisal against General Assembly agencies because of Angela Davis were the very same phenomenon. After all, the themes of "decentralization of authority," "regionalization," "participatory decision-making," and "accountability" are explicable as PR olive branches offered to the mistrustful church membership. The new organization was billed throughout the period following 1965, recall, as a responsive organization, brimming over with accountability. *"We* know who pays the bills. *You* do. We know how you feel about James Forman and Angela Davis. Well, we won't let it happen again."

But as the new organization began to function, Presbyterians shortly discovered that the theme words were not some concessionary code, as they had been in the period of adopting the reorganization proposals. The theme words belonged in the new organization as guiding principles; they had a specific meaning. They were not pointed toward anything as political as a fight. They were pointed in the other direction: as principles to be implemented in the design of a streamlined, efficient, and rational organization. The confounding irony appears again. The reorganizational effort grew a life of its own; once in place as an actual organization, it tried to function in independence of existing denominational dynamics although it insists all along that it is the very incarnation of the Presbyterian spirit.

The Final Fruits of Trivialization—PBE

The new organization has been called a "matrix model."[67] It gets its shape and understands itself in terms of what the church is in business to do, what it wants to accomplish. Obviously, anything as complex as a church has a variety of objectives, some contradictory. A good organization, accordingly, will have made some sense out of the variety of objectives by carefully determining the most important overall objectives, then arranging the objectives of lesser importance in the framework of the most important objectives.

In the old organization, for instance, there were four mission units, graded as to authority.

General Assembly = home office
Synods = liaison facility
Presbyteries = regional offices
Local Churches = outlets

Each unit has a job which comes from its location in the hierarchy. Local people sell, regional people coordinate, the home office decides. The new organization wants to discover the tasks which all four units share and then understand the units' relationships in those task terms. The new organization therefore spreads the four mission units laterally, as partners in mission. The use of *higher* and *lower* is preserved, but stripped of their hierarchical denotations. In this scheme, *higher* means more encompassing, *lower* means more local. Authority comes from the tasks, not the location of the performer of the tasks. The ideology of self-determination seems to be near at hand.

This organizational model is similar to management-by-objectives models which American business was infatuated with for awhile in the fifties. But there is one important difference. In the business model there are concrete incentives offered the employee-performers, such as bonuses, promotions, salary raises—all stemming from the presumed increased profits the increased efficiency was supposed to produce. In the church, however, the performers are at least one-half volunteer, by definition. According to Presbyterian law, an exact parity between clergy and laity is maintained in all four mission units. The lay persons are not employees; they give their time to the church free. The other half are almost entirely clergy related to parishes which set tasks that will always have precedence over larger church organizational tasks. The only people in the church model eligible to be motivated by incentives are staff persons at Synod and General Assembly levels, and to a slight extent at presbytery level. They may all be in the same mission business, but the absolute numbers of these units are staggeringly disparate: 8,742 local churches; 162 presbyteries; 17 synods; 1 General Assembly. These figures suggest that the vast majority of the organizational performers will have to be motivated to enter the new arrangement and make it work by something other than the rational incentives a business can hold out to its employees.

To an *absolute* extent, the new organization has had to engage in a nonstop pedagogical effort aimed at producing insight as the equivalent to the incentives a business can offer. The assumption of the pedagogy is that Presbyterians on seeing their mission will do it, and will prefer doing it in an efficient and rational way. The "churchwide planning process" is primarily a pedagogical device, whatever else it may be. The goals of planning are: discovery, clarification, and through them mobilization. This does not solve the problem of motivation, however, if the pedagogical planning can be considered a more or less preferred leisure-time activity. The planning will not do its stuff if people do not come to the meetings. There must be authority someplace which *requires* planning, an authority similar to the authority of business to tell its employees to do it or get fired.

The authority in the new organization is located in the church's decision to install a churchwide planning process. First, commissioners at Rochester, then commissioners at Denver, but also two-thirds of the presbyteries voted in favor of it (as well as all the other reorganization proposals, of course). The authority is constitutional —as maximum as Presbyterians can manage. No mission unit has an option to, or not to, participate, and this is as close as the new organization can get to motivation, or about as close as public school education. The child is required to attend. After that, it is up to the child and the school—a singular difference between requirement and motivation which church planning experts have blurred. In their minds requirement comes to the same thing as motivation; the reason is the planning process *will* work.

As to the process itself, it is called planning, budgeting, and evaluation, from which it gets its distinctive title: PBE. These three crucial activities of an integral system move cyclically through four stages. One full turn of the process is described in these terms:[68]

Summary	Products

Phase One—BUILDING A FRAME OF REFERENCE

recognizing who we are and why, what we have been doing, and what we face	a. Shared Insights and Common Understandings about who we are as a part of Christ's Church b. a statement of Judicatory Responsibilities c. a list of Current and Emerging Needs and Issues

Phase Two—SHAPING OUR WORK/SETTING DIRECTIONS

describing all we are involved in and setting targets	d. a Descriptive Framework (an organized tool for seeing all that is being done) e. stated Goals, Objectives, and Priorities

Phase Three—DESIGNING PROJECTS AND BUDGET

choosing what to do and budgeting to do it; deciding how to measure	f. a list of Projects to be implemented, with criteria for evaluation and with responsibilities assigned g. a Budget allocating financial and personnel resources

Phase Four—REFLECTING/APPRAISING

looking at what has been done, evaluating it, and identifying changes that need to be made	h. a Narrative Report, including questions raised, insights gained, judgements made i. Recommendations for changes in future work

At the end of phase four, you return to phase one and do it again, and so on until the *parousia*.

The style of presentation, punctuation, capitalization of process terms, no less than the offhanded PBE dialect, reveal that this is not a sophisticated *operational* system. Rigid, yes, but neither sophisticated nor complex. Its triviality tends to bowl one over.

As to the "churchwide," each unit goes through the full PBE process and the units too, in what are termed *bi-level consultations.* The greatest virtue of these consultations is to clarify specific judicatory responsibilities; this is the area of the fabled "overlap" and "duplication" so much used to sell the new organization. Clearly this is but one outcome of many. The adjacent units consider the work between them, plan, budget, and evaluate in the manner prescribed by the four-stage process. The interunit PBE requirements implement what is called the "connectional" nature of Presbyterian polity. Once upon a time "connectional" meant that the authority of the church ascended in magnitude from lower to higher judicatory. In the new organization "connectional" means the units are bonded together by the planning process they mutually use.

The General Assembly is one more judicatory in this set-up and no more than that. Its specific character is that its judicatory responsibilities are national in scope. No longer is it the visible institutionalized presence of the national UPCUSA. There is now something even broader and more comprehensive, though less visible: the reality of churchwide, that is, the sum of what all the mission units are and do, plus the sum of their relationships. To be sure, the General Assembly has final authority and stated constitutional powers, but since it instituted the churchwide planning process and *it* requires the General Assembly to participate in bi-level consultations, requires the General Assembly to accept nominations from the synods for General Assembly agency boards, there is a definite way in which PBE is outside the General Assembly's objective jurisdiction.

This is how it works. The old General Council of the General Assembly has been renamed the General Assembly Mission Council and given total administrative jurisdiction over the entire General Assembly-level operation. The new arrangement of agencies, councils, with their elected boards, is under direct GAMC supervision. The task of installing PBE throughout the church and throughout the agencies and councils, and throughout the GAMC itself, is housed in the GAMC. Its overall title is "planning," and it has three separate sections, gaining their titles from the P, B, and E. Four senior executives and a full staff at their service have done the installing. Their mandate comes directly from the constitution. They are politically invulnerable. The situation is similar to the security procedures installed by a bank. Once installed, members of the bank staff, including the president, cannot escape the demands of the procedures. The PBE managers would consider that a pejorative comparison, no doubt. They feature themselves as enablers, helpers, for whom invulnerability is nothing at all.

It should also be noted that the PBE facility in the GAMC, like the GAMC itself, is financially invulnerable. This comes about because of a sturdy and honorable tradition of Presbyterian polity which insists that self-government in the church costs money. Therefore the local churches pay for the essential ecclesiastical functions of presbyteries, synods, and the General Assembly by way of a "per capita apportionment." It really is an assessment. In an informative definition, Stated Clerk Thompson recently wrote that "ecclesiastical" denotes "those functions essential to the continuance of a judicatory"—in obvious distinction from "mission programs and projects . . . which the judicatory undertakes by its decision-making functions as a judicatory."[69] These latter expenses are supported by gifts. The General Assembly portion of the "per capita apportionment" which the local churches have to pay or else[70] goes in part to pay for the GAMC and the PBE. They are happily not in the present budget meat grinder. Their funding is secure.

After eighteen months of operation the GAMC's report to the Louisville Assembly included some instructive reflections, redefinitions, and a clarification or two. The pedagogical component is still going strong, for instance:

> GAMC has the responsibility to establish and coordinate a churchwide PBE system, and to engage in and operate a PBE process for the General Assembly as a judicatory of the church. The idea for the PBE system emerged in the reorganization at a time when the church was ready to move on to some new tasks together. It is developing as a tool by which our wide variety of ministries can be planned, budgeted, and evaluated in newly-connected ways.[71]

PBE puts on the mantle of school teacher and instructs the church on how PBE came into existence and how well it is developing. This instruction has almost the character of "Once upon a time the church asked itself, 'How can we move on together toward some new tasks?' and someone answered, 'PBE.' " The instruction ignores history, of course, but in the interests of PBE's pedagogical intent, which is to produce insight.

Then something new emerges:

> Essentially the processes of planning, budgeting, and evaluating are resources for decision-making and oversight.

This *oversight* is an old-fashioned Presbyterian word. It means the authority to advise, counsel, and censure—tied directly to the old-fashioned meaning of judicatory, which is, court. Throughout most of Presbyterian history, the best all-purpose synonym for oversight could have been "snooping." Judicatories have the authority to look into suspicious, divisive, immoral, or irregular conduct on the part of lower judicatories or individuals and then make judgments in case wrongdoing is discovered. A variety of censures may be employed, the biggest of which is excommunication from the denomination. Short of judicial proceedings, oversight means advice and counsel. It is thus quite a surprise to see the ever-rational, value-neutral PBE moving into the oversight business.

> Also these processes deal with the whole life and mission of a judicatory, as well as the totality of the life and mission of the UPC.

Not only will oversight be coming up as a new PBE resource, but its scope will be no less than the totality of Presbyterian life. This is a quantum jump; to make it possible there must be something posited theoretically between the integral planning process, now become process*es,* and Presbyterian life-in-its-totality. The link is the body of Christ, which as a body has processes, and so on.

> PBE as a system alone is nothing. As a way of enabling the Mission Council to promote and cultivate the spiritual welfare of the whole church in its world context, PBE can be useful. As faith without work is dead, so planning, budgeting, and evaluating without content is dead. Fresh, meaningful ideas must flow through the church's body processes or the church dies. Either the Spirit is in the system or the system does not live.

It is to these concerns that the development of the PBE system must turn its attention in the year ahead.

PBE must have something to offer beyond the mere dry bones of decision-making, in the same way that faith must have works. What could this something more be? "Fresh and meaningful ideas" to send pulsing through the church's body (of Christ) processes. As the body *of Christ* the church is a spiritual fellowship, but as the *body* of Christ it is an organism with a series of biological processes. What PBE could have to offer in the beyond-faith category, then, would be related to the organic processes of the church's life. This is at the same time another way of saying, "Either the Spirit is in the system or the system does not live." Fresh and meaningful ideas and Spirit are in this respect identical: withdraw either one and the system dies. They are identical in another respect: PBE is their channel and enabler. Skating perilously close to the treacherous ice of blasphemy, these theological efforts represent the clumsy attempts of process engineers to figure out a way to state the relationship between organizational process and life process because they intend to move closer to the life processes of the church. It will be interesting to see if PBE does better with life than it has done with organization.

PBE is the glamorous novelty which requires the use of new rather than revised when referring to the Presbyterian organization. Without PBE it is about the same organization: the names of its program, support, and service functions changed here and there, administrative relationships changed here and there, the whole old thing that it used to be thrown into the blender of name-change which the PBE dialect requires. Without PBE it is the same organization. This is like saying that without Watergate the Nixon-Ford administration is like other administrations.

PBE is an admitted, *confessed* theory. Its operatives consider it a sophisticated theory. It isn't. Here are its assumptions: 1. Presbyterians are rational creatures. 2. There are visible connections between "who we are" and "what our tasks are," that is, there is stability between statements of mission, judicatory responsibilities, and the Current and Emerging Needs and Issues list. 3. New ways of "looking" will jolt loose old ways of thinking. 4. The more rational a decision, the better it will be. 5. PBE is a rational process.

These assumptions in turn depend on a deeper and more important assumption: that the church is similar to a large and complex business operation, or a large and complex governmental operation.[72] It is to the end of constantly having to justify the basic assumption that PBE's theoretical efforts most often are directed. It is always having to demonstrate that it is indeed efficient, streamlined, fat-free, and up-to-date.[73] Its operatives have conducted what amounts almost to a vendetta against the old style; it seeks to obliterate all traces of the old way, to demonstrate its place in the wave of the future.

Had PBE been required to sustain the likelihood that any of its assumptions were correct as the condition for being accepted by the church, it couldn't have made the grade. None of PBE's assumptions are sustainable, especially the basic one. It has an apparently new, apolitical, value-free way of looking at the church as though it were a business or governmental operation. PBE with more reason and more chance of success would better have looked at the church as a political party, or a fairly large and disorganized lunatic asylum,[74] or, better, as a nonstop sandlot football game being played without benefit of referee. The rational analogues between the church and these kinds of "models" would be probably trite and would probably present planning process with insuperable theoretical problems, but their virtue would consist of their real base in what the church actually is. The rational analogues could not avoid being contaminated with the feeling of combat, whackiness, and authentic passion—which are the stuff of the *real* UPCUSA.

The new organization went out of its way to avoid strictly political judgments. Even though crippled from the first hour of its existence by an extraordinarily political boycott, it refused to "see" boycott and chose to "see" "changing stewardship patterns."[75] To its credit the new organization has begun to come out of the haven of its naiveté and make some extraprocess, directly political moves. It is unfortunately not very good at politics and has done so much, unfortunately, to debase language that it can scarcely hope to get a fair hearing, but it is now trying, at least.

Two GAMC meetings in the midst of the Louisville Assembly represent the nadir of PBE enthusiasm.[76] The budget situation was appalling, and the council members weren't supposed to be appalled. They decided after a lot of agonized discussion to do something about it; they would make a straight appeal to the commissioners later in the assembly, not as another mission unit, but as the one and only heavyweight champion judicatory of the church. Toward that end a committee was appointed to put together a plan for action. The committee met between these two meetings of the council and hammered out the rough draft of an appeal for funds. It was to have a preamble, referred to by the committee members as "the what God calls us to do thing," a statement of the trouble, "missionaries, hungry kids, hospitals and so on," and finally a "grabber" of some sort. The grabber they thought of is "covenant." "We're all in a covenant community; we've covenanted with God and each other to do all this mission stuff." They decided then to reserve the last morning of the assembly for a "covenanting" service. The essence of the "covenant" would be that each commissioner would go home and try to make sure that all local church pledges to the General Assembly General Mission would be paid in 1974, in addition to which there would be a concentrated personal effort on the part of all commissioners to get every local church to commit itself to a special gift to the General Mission, above existing pledges, in an amount of one dollar per church member. This was to be an appeal: a regular old arm-twisting, loyalty to the church is loyalty to God, down-home, stewardship stomp, and not the planning process at all.

The council heard the plan, looked at the rough draft of the appeal, and approved it. Then they chose Rev. Clinton Marsh, past moderator of the General Assembly, a black man who has an exciting way of preaching, to make the appeal. He ran it out—the covenant business, the what-God-calls-us-to-do business, the hungry-kids business—with great effect. The effect was that the new word about to be ruined is *covenant.* Clinton Marsh is believable; he enjoys genuine respect in the church. But he was not believable as the GAMC's idea of what the assembly would accept. It was a transparent ruse.

This particular moment captures fittingly all the elements of the mediocrity toward which the denomination started heading in 1965. God calls us to give more money.

Honorary Girls

It is somewhat easier now, after following the dizzy tailspin of language into near utter insignificance, to see how Presbyterians can with straight faces contrive to tell themselves that "God calls" them to give more money. We have now learned that they do not mean anything in particular when they say "God" or "calls," but that they are very serious about the meaning of "money" and want to go out of their way, if necessary, to explain exactly what money means— to every Presbyterian, every commissioner, and every hesitant pledger in the denomination.

The Presbyterian church has been a leader in many areas of social concern. It was a champion of education in the early days of the republic, for instance. More recently it has assumed leadership in the field of ecumenicity. On occasion it was fairly close to being a leader in the civil rights movement. And even in heading backwards, it continues to lead, now into misorganization, financial insanity, and gray funk. Surely Presbyterians are the acknowledged leaders of the entire ecclesiastical world in the matter of not meaning *anything* when they talk.

But at the end we are left with an enigma. We now know something at least about *what* happened to the UPCUSA during the last decade, but we may still be excused for being perplexed. Nothing is quite certain. The public records are so equivocal, you see. It is like picking up mercury.

Yes, *one* thing is certain. No one else knows. I refer especially to instant pundits, with their fondness for overall grand-meaning statements. "All the churches are entering a period of stabilization," they say, as though they actually knew for a fact. Sometimes they say, "The pendulum has started swinging the other way," and seem to be asserting that once it starts moving, there is no stopping it. And at times they say, "The mainline churches are trying to recover their religious bases." Dean Kelley says that, for instance. He adds that as a strategem for survival, recovering your religious bases is doomed.

They don't really know what they are talking about from their vantage points atop mountains higher even than Olympus. At least, to be exact, they don't know enough about Presbyterians to make such total statements. Presbyterians in the flesh are very much more unpredictable and less a homogeneous group than they appear as "members" of a "mainline church." For instance, Presbyterians are swinging to the right, swinging to the left, and many are stone still. How can it be said that they are "swinging the other way," in a ponderous pendulumlike movement? And if Presbyterians are entering a period of "stabilization," it will be interesting to discover what their chaos looks like.

These considerations reveal a latent point regarding the quality and identification of the term *Presbyterians*. The majority of Presbyterians have not been mentioned in this essay. I judge them to be the vast majority although I would be hard put to prove it. We have been concerned with liberals, conservative-evangelicals, staff, pastors, elders, moderators, stated clerks, leaders, committees, judicatories, but not "your average pooped-out Presbyterians." It is quite an oversight.

One such disarmingly average church member told me that he can't imagine programs or some new emphasis that could possibly mean anything at any level of his life as an individual, or as a consumer, or as a citizen. He thinks he is representative of all Presbyterians because all the Presbyterians he knows feel the same way. So, self-consciously taking upon himself the job of representing the "real Presbyterian majority," he noted what is on its mind. The split between the haves and the have-nots has worsened, to begin with. This troubles him. In spite of everything the country and church have done, the situation has become more demanding. He looked at the pollution crisis turning, then, into an energy crisis and threw up his hands. He expressed no doubt that the country would lose, no matter if the president was impeached, resigned, or stayed in office. It was one more no-win situation. His family life and that of his friends was, according to him, "a big fat bore." He confessed that he had found that being a loving, caring, Bible-believing, and Bible-teaching Presbyterian Christian is, "well, superficial. Put it this way, it's a waste of time. It's something to do because there's nothing to do." Before concluding he mused, "If the church was on the ball, it would be thinking about how people could commit a great suicide. That's what's on our minds."

Multiply this "average pooped-out Presbyterian" by about 2.8 million, each one assuming the important task of representing the majority, which in their minds equals all Presbyterian acquaintances, and suddenly the magnitude of not knowing what kind of a weirdly dissimilar group of people Presbyterians literally are appears. The real majority must be the most amused of all at the many self-confessed representatives of some majority or other.

Because pundits, quickie historians, and the new organization of the UPCUSA for their own purposes greatly oversimplify the complexity and texture of Presbyterian life, we have all the more reason to resist those procedures. The judgment can be fairly made that there are fifteen denominations in the one calling itself *the* denomination.

The enigma remains. We get nowhere trying to discover the reality of the UPCUSA in its obviously mixed membership, ranging as it does from hard-core dedicated radicals to absolute thundering neolithic conservatives; we get no further by seeking out church leaders, old and new, in order to find their thinking, garner their conclusions on what ever happened to the church. They are as perplexed as every one else.

The UPCUSA is a very public institution, and it conducts itself in public, by constitutional requirement—to such a notorious extent that the minutes and background papers of their meetings are more revealing than all the vaunted inside information enterprising snoopers might uncover about the backroom private maneuvering and deals outside the meeting halls. The UPCUSA is probably more uniquely public than any other American denomination.

A consideration on this order, of course, deepens the enigma: that such a thoroughly public institution has retreated so precipitously from its strictly institutional involvements in the life of the republic, all the while twisting language furiously in order to hide from itself the fact that a retreat has occured. The managers of the new organization, for instance, bristle at the very suggestion. It is a touchy point apparently. They prefer to think that the denomination is merely trying to achieve some symmetry between social action and "more traditional religious activities." Similarly, even conservative-evangelicals are gun-shy on this point. They want to say that social action is all right *in its place,* but that the more directly mandated activities of preaching, teaching, and evangelism must always be considered the main business of the church. In their bucolic view, the individual sinner, saved by God's grace in Jesus Christ, becomes a different kind of social being. The church's job is to change society by changing its individuals, one by one. You will not catch conservative-evangelicals admitting that society shouldn't be changed, however. All of which is so much sand in our eyes.

The UPCUSA *has* retreated; moreover, it has retreated from a once considerable and highly visible ministry to the nation into a ministry to itself. To be sure, Presbyterians at the Louisville General Assembly in 1974 maintained their commitments to Alaskans, to the

Colombian Christians involved in ROSCA, and to striking mine workers in Kentucky. They listened to Cesar Chavez but later voted in a confused parliamentary situation to withdraw their institutional commitments to his boycott. They couldn't find out how to do the good when they wanted to. And that isn't too often, these days.

In an effort to put a good face on this sad situation, Pollyanna Presbyterian enthusiasts point to the new regional synods. There. *They* show all the signs of vigorous rosey health, as indeed they should, having their funding so farsightedly protected. It is in the regional synods, however, that the great retreat can be seen with the naked eye. Self-determination, once a bold bad word spoken by the likes of Rap Brown and Angela Davis, has come home. Decision-making has gotten closer to the giver. It is the givers' mutual self-determination now being honored, as a consequence of which action projects are mounted or dropped on the basis of their "appeal" to the various church members of the synod—who pay the bills, of course.

A good face cannot be put on the situation. The existential marks of mediocrity into which the church has sunk may thus be seen finally as the marks of religion itself. Religion may well be very useful socially and very comforting privately—to such an extent that societies need religion. But publicly religion is human beings saying things they don't believe, believing things which are unbelievable, hating for the sake of love, sacrificing intelligence, lying for the sake of truth, and fighting social change in the name of a glorious past. The rhetoric advocating the return of ecclesiastical authority to local levels, for all its democratizing ring, sounds like something else: the return of a denomination from its institutional location in the modern world of institutions to the religious atmosphere of the sanctuary, where reconciliation can be understood and where, furthermore, it is said to work.

C-67 made a heroic effort to shove reconciliation into the nonreligious world "out there," but it was ill-considered. Reconciliation is totally innocent of knowledge about institutions and impersonal battle. It has nothing to propose but *ultimate* acts of loving sacrifice, which happen to be beside the point of impersonal conflicts.[77] The Vietnam War did not end because reconciliation-inspired individuals immolated themselves. The energy crisis is not eased by the decision of religiously convicted people to forsake their automobiles. At best these are the feeble attempts of the truly religious to introduce personal and interpersonal considerations into situations which by definition don't recognize them.

Reconciliation always did belong in the sanctuary, manifested in beautifully wrought leather Bibles, golden crosses, lovely music, and moist-eyed Christian love. And this refocuses attention on the original decision to lump the whole gospel into the one term which *could not* by nature reach the terrifying world of forces and trends, of nameless, faceless movements, of violence and inhuman destruction. Said this way, the retreat was no less than following reconciliation back to where it belongs. Clearly, the theological attempt to *define* the church as an agency of reconciliation in the contemporary world has proved itself a flop, whether or not the church ever could *be* that agency.

Well, should it be counted a surprise that a *church,* a religious organization after all, has begun to reemphasize its strictly religious character? Obviously not, were the UPCUSA the kind of strictly religious organization which can simply chew up language at will and practice its interpersonal chumminess with Jesus Christ without anyone caring or noticing. The surprise—more like outright perplexity—arises because *this* denomination once so proudly declared that its religion was forcing it out into the impersonal world there to honor its religious commitments to God's justice and love. So, when it retreats, dissembling all the while that it isn't really retreating, perplexity, well, *burgeons.*

This much appears to be clear. Something has to give. The UPCUSA cannot claim to be a contemporary mission-minded organization and at the same time confine its mission to its own members and those happy others who may at any moment—owing to a terrific evangelical effort—convert. There is something like a choice involved; that the choice must be made is something like an issue.

Before choosing the denomination would do well to inspect carefully the place it has retreated to. It is, of course, the church. It is a warm, homelike, nuclear-family-like, protected bedroom and kitchen-like place into which James Forman and Angela Davis burst as invaders from Mars. Well, this place bears a striking resemblance to another place: the place Elizabeth Janeway identifies as the obligatory sphere into which women have been cast. She distinguishes this place from "man's world," which women may not enter, at least not as willful, self-determining, free, all-around human beings.[78] "The church has no business in politics" just naturally finds an analogue in "Women's place is the home." What the church and women do in their "place" is the trivial, boring, necessary but necessarily *secondary* tasks of nurture and support. To be "feminine" and to be "religious" amount to the same thing: to be banned from anything real and important. The brilliant theologian, Dr. Beverly Harrison, has made this point with devastating clarity. She says the church has been "feminized," and offers for consideration:

> I never cease to be amazed that few notice the similarities between the worst features of the dominant Protestant clergyman's stereotype and those characteristics thought to be intrinsic to woman's nature—sentimentality, indirectness of communication and moralizing, ambivalence and inconsistency of principle, preference for anecdotal rather than analytic thinking, fear of conflict, and a need to please and to be loved at any cost. Similarity of character, I submit, is largely a similarity of social location.[79]

The shock of recognition! Of course. It is an irony that the UPCUSA in feminizing itself continues to mouth the brave platitudes of male supremacy, but in the end the recognition cannot be withstood. The UPCUSA as a corporate entity must be counted *honorary girls* in the American society, thus ending with the worst of both worlds: bemused condescension from the inhabitants of man's world and disgust from the women just now waging a momentous fight with male supremacy.

Once there may have been plenty of reason to preserve and celebrate the authentic values of interpersonal intimacy *in* the world of institutional racism and sexism, where, that is, such a witness actually counts. A good case could be made for always doing that. But to have siezed on the interpersonal intimacy while relinquishing the field of combat with impersonal institutional forces, trends, movements, and so on is the feature of the retreat that is so unbelievable it defies caricature. Who is the real victim of character defamation when the UPCUSA is called an honorary girl, the church or women?

The denomination will certainly not want to view its present situation in these terms. What denomination would? I think of no denomination, however, which has not, one way or another, made the same retreat into the safer and more traditionally feminine regions of American society—not that they were ever very far out there in the world. The Episcopalians, for instance, are not just retreating, they are *scrambling,* as they seek some way to get eleven women priests unordained. The irony is almost confounding. And judging recent expostulations of other official Protestant bodies on their *religious* role in American society (definitely *not* political-institutional), and their tender regard for the primary needs of their own memberships (including the need to send a few dollars now and then to the starving), I can almost believe I am hearing Presbyterians talk. At this point there is a clear Protestant-Christian consensus. No one is out there; all the denominations are safely at-home.

In suggesting that the UPCUSA faces an issue because it has a choice to make, I am asserting my own personal optimism, which is unsupported by the facts. The facts suggest that the UPCUSA already *is* a trivial institution, stuck in the dank backwaters of mere religion by self-conscious choice. The choice has already been made. It was being made in the reconciliation decision, the "Design for Mission" decision, the reorganization decision, the churchwide planning process decision, the 100 percent–65 percent decision, the budget reprisal decision, and in dozens of other less significant decisions. The wages of trivialization *is* triviality. The retreat *has* been made, and so on. These are the publically arrived at, publically constituted facts. They are a pretty feeble support for optimism, in spite of which I am nonetheless optimistic, or at least hopeful, that Presbyterians can see they have a choice, hence face a live issue.

My optimism is grounded in a twenty-five-year-long acquaintance with the very Presbyterians who suffer the denomination's inanities so patiently (some of them trying to think of a great way to commit suicide) and listen in numbed silence to the chatter of fanatics and fools. They are a people equally capable of enormous generosity and indefinite tolerance for banality. The move is theirs to make, to the extent a move can be made. They are the institution, after all, leaders and the led together. And if they decide that their problem hasn't been organizational and isn't now organizational, but frankly theological, then they will have struggled sufficiently out of their ennui to recommence a fierce debate about the shape of faithfulness to God in the contemporary world—something hauntingly similar to the matter encountered by the drafting committee as it thought about how to arrange a contemporary confession of faith, it appears.

The optimism exists, moreover, despite the presence of vociferous conservative-evangelicals in the denomination who have made most of the noise and seem surest that the theological debate was settled when the last word of the New Testament was written. I'll tell you about those conservative-evangelicals. They are a small contingent of Presbyterians whose ability to shout very loudly makes them appear to be an army. This can be documented. You would think from their open assertions that the budget reprisal was their idea and their doing. I have checked it out. I selected the names of twenty-three familiar and readily identifiable conservative-evangelical churches. I looked at their statistical performance and discovered that while the denomination as a whole was reducing General Mission giving 32 percent in 1967–73, these churches reduced theirs by 49 percent. Abstracting the really hard-core conservative-evangelical churches from these twenty-three, the reduction was 75 percent. It is astonishing that the total amounts are so paltry; only $309,000 of the total drop is accounted for by these churches.[80] One would think from a close reading of the *Presbyterian Layman* that the boycott was an exclusive conservative-evangelical revolt, and this thinking would rest on two facts: the overall size of the budget reprisal and the open truculence of these conservative-evangelicals. The statistical study shows the very opposite; the truculence can only be correlated to a small portion of the total drop.

It appears to me like one of the greatest shills in church history, whose ethics make the Angela Davis caper seem honorable by comparison. We see all this fog besetting the church, hear all this sick populist noise, hear so many Jesus Christs it would seem we were in a Methodist revival, only to discover that the fog is not a general climatic condition, sent from On High, but is coming out of a tiny fog machine located in the church basement. Clearly, conservative evangelicals are not the ones responsible for the shill, even though they are delighted to believe they have forced the denomination to repudiate its affair with Angela Davis, and to tighten its belt generally. The shill artists are the reorganization committees, which used conservative evangelical concerns as a launching pad for PBE—a fact some conservative evangelicals are just now beginning to understand.

Yes, despite even the presence of a certain vociferous cell of Presbyterians who fundamentally want to repeal the twentieth century—as a prelude to reinstalling the Bible as the verbally inspired and utterly inerrant Word of God, and *that* as a prelude to preaching the plain Word to lost sinners—I remain optimistic. Despite the low estate into which public theological conversation has sunk, I remain optimistic that it can be revived. Despite the appeal of religious retreat, I remain optimistic that the plain ugly problems of a late twentieth-century world will prevail over every obscurantism and force the church to face them. Despite the badly battered condition of reconciliation, I remain optimistic that it can be reconstituted and reused as a meaningful theological term. Despite the pall PBE has cast on language, I remain optimistic that language will counter-attack and reassert its primordial self against all technicalizing trivialization.

Perhaps my optimism is insupportable, in which case we may expect the UPCUSA to die soon. I suggest, however, .hat you should not count Presbyterians hopeless or make the funeral arrangements until you literally hear the last gasp. They will surprise you.

Notes

1. I shall use the initials in place of the name throughout the essay, an ugliness for which I may be forgiven in consideration of the number of times the name of the denomination appears. I shall also use Presbyterian to mean United Presbyterian; this is not a slight on those Presbyterians who are members of the Presbyterian Church in the U.S.—the southern church— who are Presbyterian but not United Presbyterian; it is a proleptic recognition of the proposed reunion of the two churches.

2. To the extent that just behind doing stands intentionality to do, phenomenologists join existentialist and analytic philosophers in this perfectly modern consensus; modern here means Hegel and onwards. The phenomenologist M. Wertheimer, for instance: "A thing which is black and uncanny is just as uncanny as it is black, yea, if it is both at the same time, it is uncanny in the first place." This is cited by Ulrich Sonnemann, *Existence and Therapy* (New York: Grune and Stratton, 1954), p. 17. What makes it modern, as opposed to classical philosophical reflection, is the renunciation of routes to being qua being before, or as the ground of, doing. What being "discloses" is another matter, however.

3. Edward Dowey, Jr., *A Commentary on the Confession of 1967 and an Introduction to the Book of Confessions* (Philadelphia: Westminster Press, 1968) p. 40.

4. The cited material comes from the Confession, 9.06. It is the Confession *of 1967,* and this attracts attention to the historical confessions which the UPCUSA included in its contemporary confessional act: the Apostles' Creed; the Nicene Creed; the Scots Confession; the Heidelberg Catechism;

the Second Helvetic Confession; the Westminster Confession; the Barmen Confession. The reaffirmation of this considerable and comprehensive confessional material relieved Presbyterian confessors of the necessity to cover the entire space between alpha and omega.

5. Ibid.

6. The Confession is very clear that God is a masculine being for whom the masculine pronoun is required. The Confession is convinced also that while mankind may very well be composed of males and females, members of mankind are invariably "men," or, if one, is "man." I have been schooled by rigorous theological students who are also women to avoid in my own writing the use of automatic masculine terms to refer to beings whose sexuality is in dispute, unknown, or mixed. But I have made no attempt to fix up the writing of the confessors or to cleanse the idiom of their writing in discussing it. It is, as will become evident, sexist all the way.

7. In referring to the Confession of 1967 as C-67, I follow a practice adopted by many Presbyterian publications and by most disputants.

8. Barmen Confession, article II, paragraph 3.

9. Dowey, *Commentary,* p. 40.

10. This and following quotations are cited from C-67, II.A.4, paragraphs 9.44–9.47.

11. Dowey, *Commentary,* p. 128. Dowey writes, "At the end of each of the . . . paragraphs is a self-condemnation of the church by the church. It resembles in some ways the anathema lists of heretics in older creeds and confessions, or the negative theses of the Barmen Declaration. They are a magnifying mirror for individual and group self-examination."

12. When it is reported on p. 71 that the General Mission giving was $30,999,669, that figure should be seen to represent the total giving of churches to the General Mission. The $39 million figure I quote here includes the gifts from churches, and also the gifts of individuals and special organizations, such as the United Presbyterian Women.

13. The Presbytery of San Diego submitted an Overture to the 1972 General Assembly calling for a one-year suspension of the reorganization process while a special committee of thirty-five, elected by the Presbyteries, carefully restudied the whole matter. The reasons for this action were contained in a preamble. It is a good example of the conspiratorial view of the role of board staff: "There has been in recent years the development of two parallel governments in the church, namely, the official judicatory government and the *de facto* government exercised by the boards and agencies of the General Assembly. . . . The judicatory government of the church is more directly related to the local churches and their opinions and needs. . . . It has been increasingly difficult for judicatories to exercise control over the bureaucratic government of the church because this second government by its very nature controls the public relations media of the church and employs

persons who devote their entire time to campaigning for judicatory acceptance of bureaucratic decisions, while commissioners to judicatories can be only part-time church politicians. . . . Recent attempts to resolve the problem, notably the recent reorganization of the boards and agencies and the proposal for Regional Synods have resulted in making even more difficult the control of boards and agencies by the judicatories." From the *General Assembly Minutes,* 1972, part I, pp. 54–5.

14. This statement was made in an interview during which Ramage recounted the early, pre-1965, reorganization effort. "Radical evil" for him meant the nearly invincible *arrangement* of social, political, and economic forces which one encounters in a metropolitan area. The forces are each one narrowly seeking some particular goals; the term *evil* becomes necessary when the forces coalesce, often forsaking narrow self-interest; the evil becomes "radical" when it puts away normal intractibility to social change and aggressively seeks to thwart it. That's what Ramage thinks we must become appropriately sophisticated about.

15. *Presbyterian Layman,* August, 1973.

16. Showalter made this statement to me in his church's parking lot after I had addressed one of the groups in the Libertyville Presbyterian Church in 1967. It was a dispassionate statement of fact, in his telling.

17. Dean Kelley, *Why Conservative Churches Are Growing* (New York: Harper & Row, 1972), p. 17.

18. Ibid., pp. 145–46.

19. Ibid., p. 146.

20. Ibid., pp. 134–38.

21. I do not intend to criticize Kelley for offering the explanation. In his defense it should be noted that he has taken on himself the task of telling mainline churches what really is wrong and what they will have to do in order to return to rosey health, or, failing that, what will stabilize a terminal illness. At many places in his book he explicitly states that the organizational counsel is not his personal advice, and by that seems to be saying that his personal advice would be of a different order. That is a delicate line to be preserving, however, when he describes with rather more passion than is called for the "conservative function of religion"; also his lumping of a lot of aggressive contemporary urban ministry into the category of "technological service" betrays an understanding of "fact" that is less value-free than he claims to be. I think he thinks the church should attend to religion in the full realization that most religion turns out to be an enemy of social change —a realization that does not diminish just because he can also assert that if religion sponsors social change authentically, so much the better.

22. Robert Townsend, *Up the Organization* (New York: Knopf, 1970), p. 142. Townsend is saying that you can't motivate people, *that* is the door locked on the inside. My license for using his locale to describe this religious

unhappiness is that it is the same door, same lock, and same inside. It is an expression of my disbelief in encountering any discussion of religious phenomena which confuses facticity with phenomenal location. Professional phenomenologists of religion identify phenomena within a field of methodological determinants and are comfortable in describing such things as the experience of the holy. Psychologists of religion locate religious phenomena within their own field of methodological determinants and are comfortable describing such things as shame, gratitude, joy; they are emotional concretions related to the religious situation—formally defined. Sociologists of religion, however, identify the function of religion in society and move from that point backwards into the religious person for data. Standing myself in the company of persons who may be said to have had religious experience, I am amazed at these various professional expressions of unwillingness to *expect* deception, ignorance, or outright error at the source of all this data, namely, the religious person standing on the other side of a self-locked door. And who is to know the difference?

23. From a statistical summary found in the *General Assembly Minutes* 1974, part II, p. 737.

24. *Presbyterian Layman,* August, 1973. This quotation appears in the published speech of Paul Cupp to the first national convention of the Presbyterian Lay Committee in June, 1973, in Grove City, Pennsylvania. The publication is obviously put out by the organization. It is said, by the committee, to have a circulation of 340,000, but it is sent without benefit of subscription to some Presbyterian ministers and perhaps to others.

25. Ibid., same speech.

26. Still the same speech, but this portion, omitted by the *Presbyterian Layman,* appears in *A.D.* magazine, September, 1973, in a report of the convention filed by UPC editor, James Gittings. *A.D.* is the magazine which continues *Presbyterian Life* and the *United Church Herald.*

27. The Presbyterian Church in the U.S. (southern) at this writing is in the draft document stage of its modern confessional statement. It is organized around and fascinated by "the story." I freely predict its authors will regret the decision. The PCUS conservative-evangelicals—the ones who have not yet left the church—will eat the drafting committee alive.

28. This is represented as being the conservative-evangelical position by a member of the Lay Committee's Board of Directors, Dr. Charles MacKenzie, Jr., in a published speech, *Presbyterian Layman,* August, 1973.

29. I quote from the transcript of a tape recording of a speech made by Rev. Leon Fanniel, executive director of the General Assembly Mission Council until July, 1974, to the General Assembly on Saturday morning, June 22, 1974. The groan to which I refer was "audible and widespread" in the vicinity of the microphone which was located on one of the press tables, which qualifies the "widespread" somewhat. But I stick by my asser-

tion that the groan was uniquely and generally Presbyterian.

30. From the *Presbyterian Life* coverage of the assembly, July, 1972.

31. This and following quotations from the "Design for Mission" are taken from the *General Assembly Minutes,* 1968, part I, pp. 245–90.

32. Note to non-Presbyterian readers: In old-fashioned Presbyterian organization the sessions of local churches, presbyteries, synods, and General Assembly were called judicatories, which means, courts. They were the place for making judgments, for deliberating ecclesiastical policy. Presbyterian zealots call this graded system of ecclesiastical courts, ascending in authority, a great system of self-government because representatives from the lower courts make up the higher courts. They conveniently overlook the principal intent of the courts in the first place, which was to determine the existence of, then stamp out moral turpitude. In its contemporary use judicatory means something like "governmental unit," the trend of course being toward administration.

33. I am quoting here and in following citations from the Report of the Special Committee on Restructuring General Assembly Agencies, which appears in the *General Assembly Minutes,* 1971, part I, pp. 440–506.

34. These quotations come from David Ramage's recollection of the more or less typical utterances.

35. The official committee report to the General Assembly in 1966 was a good deal more circumspect, as might be expected. It contained this representation, for instance: "The church is clearly concerned to discover more effective ways of accomplishing its mission. The extent and depth of the study given the report, in a year in which the church has also been engaged in discussion of the proposed confession, indicates the seriousness with which the church regards the matters of structure and administration referred the Committee." It is obviously an idealized representation. See *General Assembly Minutes,* 1966, part I, p. 166.

36. There should not be inferred any attempt here to elevate trivialization to the status of a grand explanatory category. It is a useful term in ethical analysis, and that is all. I got it from an Erving Goffman footnote where he describes "pencil and paper students of the self who start with a subject's verbal description of himself, often based on his selection from verbal trait-lists, instead of starting with the serious ethnographic task of assembling the various ways in which the individual is treated and treats others, and deducing what is implied about him through this treatment. The result has been a trivialization of Cooley, Mead, and social psychology." *Relations in Public* (New York: Harper Colophon, 1972) p. 342 n.

Paul Starr, a sociologist at the Yale Law School, in a New York *Times* book review, September 15, 1974, cracks down hard on fellow sociologist Charles Kadushin for compiling exact statistics about vague and imprecise information and calling it data. It is, but then again it isn't. Starr wrote: "This kind of false precision is a parody of social science. Science does not call for the trivializing of ideas, or for data that are little more than artifacts of methodology. There is no reason why a sociologist need be a menace to common logic and the English language."

From another quarter, Leszek Kolakowski lambasts lock-step Socialist sociology for confusing party loyalty with intellectual honesty. Here is one of his broadsides: "Primitive pseudo-Marxist sociology held that the entire content of these (social) theories was determined by class interests. It follows that the entire content of Marxist doctrine is determined by the interests of the working-class party. And since these interests, as another postulate has it, cannot conflict with the growth of true knowledge of the world, then everything that serves these interests is true. However, precisely what serves these interests was defined without theory and only by political decisions. Under these conditions, theory had to act on the principle that everything that is real is reasonable—an utterly trivial interpretation." *Toward a Marxist Humanism* (New York: Grove Press, 1968), p. 164.

Goffman, Starr, and Kolakowski identify a certain almost comical intellectual pretension in the procedures of trivialization, something like the advertizers of a dog food who elevated the presence of milk protein as a distinctive and superior ingredient of their product but without mentioning that milk protein is irrelevant to a dog's diet. Presbyterians, or sociologists, or Americans, or Socialists, or Socialist sociologists do not have a market on trivialization. But the trivialization I discuss is a Presbyterian phenomenon and is, as far as I can tell, unrelated to anything else, but especially *everything* else.

37. Townsend, *Up the Organization,* p. 104.

38. *A.D.* managing editor, Mayo Smith, told me that a friend of his walked into the office of a colleague in the new organization but hesitated at the door when he saw that the colleague was talking to his secretary. The colleague then is reported to have said, "Oh, it's all right. Come on in. I was just confidentializing."

39. The Mason Committee report—that is, the report of the Special Committee on Restructuring General Assembly Agencies—takes up where the Schram Committee left off and uses much of the same background material, definitions of terms, and scriptural citations. It will be clear that this and the following quotations are from the same report identified in footnote 33.

40. Note No. 2 to non-Presbyterian readers: The General Council was the administrative arm of the General Assembly between its annual meetings. It was supposed to coordinate, supervise, plan, and also handle interim items of emergency importance but in light of General Assembly policies. It was composed of high-level board and agency staff and at-large members elected by the General Assembly. The moderator was always the moderator

of the General Assembly. Naturally, the council meets during the assembly because it has responsibility for making so many administrative reports—a system of accountability, it seems.

41. Tom Wolfe, *The Electric Kool-Aid Acid Test* (New York: Farrar, Straus & Giroux, 1968), p. 175.

42. I learned of her happiness by reading an interview with her in the San Francisco *Examiner,* September 22, 1974.

43. *Presbyterian Life,* July 15, 1971. Mr. Gray is pastor of the Hamilton Union Presbyterian Church, Guilderland, New York.

44. Matthew 23:13–36.

45. *Presbyterian Life,* July 15, 1971.

46. From the *Presbyterian Layman,* September, 1971, which is reprinting an article by Rev. Lester Kinsolving in the Auburn New York *Citizen-Advertizer.* Kinsolving runs a syndicated religious column.

47. *Presbyterian Life,* February 15, 1972.

48. Note No. 3 to non-Presbyterian readers: The session is the ruling body—or judicatory—of the local church. It is composed of ruling elders (whose number is up to the congregation) who are elected by the congregation for set terms and upon satisfactory answers to constitutional questions propounded to them are ordained. The moderator of the session is the teaching elder or better known as the pastor also ordained upon satisfactory answer to mostly the same questions.

49. The COCAR statement was written September 30 and printed in *Presbyterian Life,* November 1, 1971. COCAR began as CORAR, that is, the Committee on Religion and Race. It was an early civil rights movement era effort put together by the General Assembly to broker its explicit concerns to the civil rights movement and the movement's explicit concerns to the General Assembly. In time it was elevated and standardized into a formal council. But in the elevation it didn't lose its primary function, which was to be the conscience of the denomination in so-called matters of race. This was the basic point of the COCAR statement. What received the most publicity was COCAR's refusal to admit any propriety-drop in making the Davis grant.

50. *Presbyterian Life,* July 1, 1971.

51. Ibid.

52. The arguments for the grant were no bargain either. I cite particularly the speech of a veteran black Presbyterian, Rev. Edler Hawkins, a former moderator of the General Assembly and co-chairperson of COCAR. It was defensive and a tired sort of reiteration of a justice-oriented gospel that sounds suspiciously flat, as though he didn't believe the General Assembly cared anymore. Liberal talk in 1971 was worn out, in many places other than Presbyterian meetings, of course.

53. See Sarah Bentley Doely (ed.), *Women's Liberation and the Church*

(New York: Association Press, 1971); Mary Daly, *The Church and the Second Sex* (New York: Harper & Row, 1968), and *Beyond God the Father* (Boston: Beacon Press, 1973); Rosemary Redford Reuthers (ed.), *Religion and Sexism* (New York: Simon & Schuster, 1974), and "Male Clericalism and the Dread of Women," *The Ecumenist*, 11, 5, July-August, 1973.

54. The credentials are formulated impressively by Robert McAfee Brown, *The Pseudonyms of God* (Philadelphia: Westminster Press, 1972), especially part 3. It is his long-time theological presupposition that God's *feeling* for the Assyrians used to chastise Israel has been rather underestimated by Israel, and that this *feeling* is one of virtual chumminess—a presupposition he has been elaborating all his theological life. Brown does not address the Angela Davis embroglio in his book, but there is no doubt where he would come out theologically, had he chosen to write about it.

55. *Presbyterian Outlook,* August 7, 1971. Of the 7,000 letters which had been received at the time of this report, 100 were said to be in support of the grant. There is no reason to doubt the ratio changed as more letters came in. The September 20, 1971, edition reports that the figure had grown to 10,000. And it is from this latter report that the figures on p. 50 are based, namely, that of the 1,200 letters from sessions, 200 indicated intent to divert funds from the General Mission.

56. From the John Knox Presbyterian Church, Tulsa, Oklahoma.

57. From the First Presbyterian Church, Orange, New Jersey.

58. From the First Presbyterian Church, Anaheim, California. According to the latitude recently provided local churches by the General Assembly, General Mission giving can be earmarked—"designated"—for special budget items and by agreement will not be spent on anything else.

59. From the Menlo Park Presbyterian Church, Menlo Park, California.

60. From the First Presbyterian Church, Miami, Florida.

61. From the Webster Groves Presbyterian Church, Webster Groves, Missouri.

62. *General Assembly Minutes,* 1974, part II, p. 735.

63. *General Assembly Minutes,* 1967, part I, pp. 94–95.

64. *Presbyterian Life,* July 15, 1971.

65. *Presbyterian Layman,* September, 1971. The statement comes from an article written by George Craig, an elder and lawyer.

66. The transition from the old to the new organization at the national staff level reduced staff (executive and clerical) from 1,028 to 781, according to Rev. G. Daniel Little (*A.D.,* February, 1974), director of the Budgeting Section. Although the personnel staff helped to relocate staff which was terminated and provided them with termination benefits, there was a lot of hardship. Dennis Shoemaker, writing in the *Christian Century,* March 14, 1973, makes it out to be an attack on a whole sector of the more aggressive, radical staff people in the old organization. Shoemaker claims they were the

ones fired, or, because they had the wit, had found other employment before the storm hit. The rough treatment of personnel moved James Gittings to write an editorial on the subject in *A.D.* December, 1973, entitled "Nostra Culpa." Gittings used the word *savaging* to describe what had happened.

Two points must be kept separate in this consideration. The move for an economy to be achieved by staff reduction gave the new organization an opportunity to hire staff congenial to its aims and style. That can be proved. The other, more telling, point is that by hiring women and minority group representatives in almost ostentatiously scrupulous regard for General Assembly policy, the new organization could conveniently operate an actual vendetta against the old-style bureaucrats whose penchant for controversy was well known. This point cannot be proved. Professor Jack Stotts, chairperson of the Advisory Council on Church and Society, in an interview, called the new organization's *apparent* responsiveness to third world and women "knee-jerk liberalism of the worst order," and he prophesied in June, 1974, before the fact, that when the new organization began letting people go on account of the newest budget squeeze, these would be the first to be fired. Stotts is a good predicter as well as an ace theologian.

67. I am indebted to Joe Dempsey, elder, organizational expert, and founder of The Los Angeles Inter-Foundation Center, for this term.

68. From a mimeographed document entitled "Planning, Budgeting, and Evaluating in the UPCUSA," distributed by the General Assembly Mission Council, May, 1973. It is a condensation of a longer and less precise document prepared for a planning consultation in March, 1973. Daniel Little in an interview called this stage of planning theory "primitive." As I read a more recent paper on evaluation prepared for the Louisville Assembly, which should be less "primitive" according to Little's "evaluation," I judge that there must be stages of "primitive" because the latter document simply isn't significantly different from the early document.

69. From an article Thomspon wrote for the *Presbyterian Layman,* August, 1973.

70. The stated clerk notes very carefully the mechanics of the "or else." First, the presbytery must remit on time the General Assembly's share of the per capita apportionment it collects or the presbytery's "commissioners to the next meeting of the General Assembly would be entitled only to the proportion of the per deim and mileage comparable to the portion of the per capita apportionment paid by the presbytery." The presbytery is thus motivated to keep that per capita apportionment money coming in from the local churches. "Failure of a particular church to pay its share of the per capita apportionment raises serious questions about its identity with and participation in the work of the church . . . (and) may occasionally result from incipient disloyalty to the presbytery, synod, or General Assembly.

Should such a condition be discovered, presbytery should act forthrightly." Among the things a presbytery can do is dissolve the church. Or, the "or else" is real.

71. From the report of the General Assembly Mission Council to the General Assembly, found in materials prepared for commissioners in the "Blue Book," vol. V, pp. 666 ff. Further quotations in this series come from the same source.

72. The staff person for the Mason Committee, Rev. Hugh Annett, a graduate student in business administration at the time, was said to be enamored of the organizational set-up installed by NASA. Inferences may or may not be licitly made from this fact: that the new Presbyterian organization is like the NASA organization. It is a hard inference to make because in order to make it new ways must be found to account for the fact that rockets got off the ground and flew all the way to the moon.

73. The Mission Council prepared a "Descriptive Framework" for the 1974 operational budget and presented it to commissioners at the 1974 General Assembly. It describes itself as being a "tool by means of which a judicatory can organize, describe, and interrelate every part of its program and operation." The three judicatory responsibilities for the General Assembly are: "Preparing for Mission; Doing Mission; Enabling Others to Do Mission." Beneath them are ranged program categories, and then areas of activity. But attention to the actual figures in the budget discloses that the three mission agencies' and the four councils' operating budgets have been scissored and then pasted up in a rearranged form in order to provide this new and also arbitrary way of "looking." In this instance PBE's pedagogical intent has been overpowered by its need to demonstrate, to produce, to score. It is a sales document, in short. To get significant factual information about budget items, it is necessary to rescissor the "Descriptive Framework" and repaste the pieces together—that is, to reassemble the original operational budgets of the agencies and councils.

74. Erving Goffman, op cit., appendix, "The Insanity of Place," would of course be the source of availability of this model.

75. The Mason Committee report said, for instance, "Pressures are likely to increase for more adequate financing of synod and presbytery causes as those judicatories undertake greater shares of the mission within their bounds. Stewardship patterns are already showing the difficulty of establishing priorities for national and international programs. Already national units, even in their present identity, are finding it necessary to adjust both their finances and their functions." This is like calling a riot a social adjustment.

76. The meetings were public; I attended them and tape-recorded the proceedings. I attended a portion of the appeal committee meeting also but did not tape-record its proceedings. I did, however, take notes.

84

77. See Hannah Arendt's fascinating description of Billy Budd's mute innocence in *On Revolution* (New York; Viking Press, 1965) pp. 74–83.

78. Elizabeth Janeway, *Man's World, Woman's Place* (New York: Delta Books, 1971).

79. Beverly Harrison, "Sexism and the Contemporary Church: When Evasion Becomes Complicity," in *Sexist Religion and Women in the Church,* ed. Alice L. Hageman (New York; Association Press, 1974) pp. 195-216.

80. By a close reading of the *Presbyterian Layman* since 1968, when it began publication, it is possible to determine the openly and firmly conservative-evangelical churches. I chose to select those churches in which prominent lay members of the board of directors were members, and churches whose pastors were prominent members or past-members of the board of directors. In addition I selected some churches whose pastors write regularly for the publication. I paid no attention to getting a good geographical spread but was happy to find that my selection was well-spread across the country. I paid no attention either to the size of church in making the selection and was happy again to discover that I had chosen some of the largest and some of the smallest churches in the denomination. By way of emphasizing the smallness of this fierce 49 percent drop in the General Mission giving of these twenty-three churches, it is clear that if there were 100 churches of the same ideological make-up and their giving drop were identical to the drop of the twenty-three, the overall drop for the 100 churches would be $1,344,000, or about 10 percent of the total drop of $10,896,000. Ten percent is a lot of money, it turns out; but it also turns out that 10 percent is a long way from 100 percent, and that is what the conservative-evangelical ideology is always edging toward claiming.